WARBIRD TECH SERIES

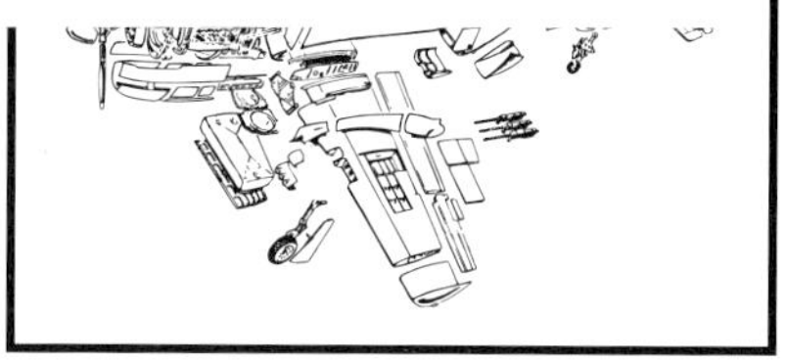

VOLUME 33

GRUMMAN
A-6 INTRUDER

BY DENNIS R. JENKINS

specialtypress
PUBLISHERS AND WHOLESALERS

COPYRIGHT © 2002 DENNIS R. JENKINS

Published by
Specialty Press Publishers and Wholesalers
39966 Grand Avenue
North Branch, MN 55056
United States of America
(800) 895-4585 or (651) 277-1400
http://www.specialtypress.com

Distributed in the UK and Europe by
Midland Publishing
4 Watling Drive
Hinckley LE10 3EY, England
Tel: 01455 233 747 Fax: 01455 233 737
http://www.midlandcountiessuperstore.com

ISBN 1-58007-050-7

All rights reserved. No part of this book may be reproduced or transmitted in any form or by any means, electronic or mechanical including photocopying, recording, or by any information storage and retrieval system, without permission from the Publisher in writing.

Material contained in this book is intended for historical and entertainment value only, and is not to be construed as usable for aircraft or component restoration, maintenance, or use.

Printed in China

Front Cover: *An A-6 (152948) returns to its aircraft carrier in July 1974. Note the split wingtip flaps and nearly full-span leading edge device. (Roy Stafford via the Mick Roth Collection)*
Back Cover (Left Top): *An A-6E (158533) from VA85 shows its colorful squadron markings. The lack of fuselage speed brakes signifies that this aircraft was a new-build E-model, not a converted A-6A. (Grumman via Mick Roth Collection)*
Back Cover (Right Top): *The A-6 could carry some unusual payloads, including the BQM-74C target drone shown here, in addition to a wide range of dumb bombs, mines, and precision-guided weapons. (U.S. Navy)*
Back Cover (Lower): *The A-6C used a large TRIM cupola to house its low-light television camera and FLIR equipment. The later A-6E TRAM benefited from several years' advancement in technology, and fit improved equipment into a small nose turret (Grumman via the Robert F. Dorr Collection)*
Title Page: *A formation of A-6Es from VA-52 while the squadron was assigned to the USS* Kitty Hawk *(CV-63). (Grumman via Mick Roth Collection)*

WARBIRDTECH SERIES

Table of Contents

Grumman A-6 Intruder

	Preface 4	
	And the Thanks go to ...	
Chapter 1	**Bucking the Trend** 5	
	The Beginning of All-Weather Attack	
Chapter 2	**The First Intruders** 13	
	1950s High Tech	
Chapter 3	**Specialized Intruders** 33	
	A Few Odd-Balls Fill Important Niches	
Chapter 4	**Flying Gas Stations** 51	
	Intruders as Tankers	
Color Section	**Intruders in Color** 65	
	Not Always Gray	
Chapter 5	**Intruders Get Better** 73	
	1970s High Tech	
Chapter 6	**The Replacement that Wasn't** 95	
	The Stillborn A-12 and A-6F	
Appendix A	**Bureau Numbers** 103	
	Rets, Bacs, Mods, and Others	
Appendix B	**Significant Dates** 104	
	Key Dates in the History of the A-6 Intruder	

Grumman A-6 Intruder

PREFACE

AND THE THANKS GO TO ...

The Grumman Iron Works, as the Grumman Corporation was affectionately known amongst Naval Aviators, supplied the majority of U.S. Navy aircraft for almost 50 years. Grumman aircraft were known to be rugged and dependable, and the aviators trusted them implicitly. Figuratively, if not literally, the EA-6B was the last product of the Grumman Iron Works. After almost 60 years of producing Navy aircraft at the Naval Industrial Reserve Facility on eastern Long Island, the newly formed Northrop Grumman shut down the plant forever. Plant 6 was over a quarter-mile long and served as the final assembly line for the A-6 series — Plant 7 served as the flight test hangar facility. Grumman's aircraft operations have moved to St. Augustine, Florida, but no new aircraft are being manufactured there — only modifications to existing airframes.

The A-6 ran counter to most aircraft of its era. Bigger, faster, and higher were the buzzwords of the day. The Intruder was none of these — it was slow, pudgy, and ugly. Although the Intruder would never win a beauty contest, it was capable of lifting a substantial amount of ordnance and delivering it on target, day and night, in virtually any weather. As an attack aircraft it served in two major conflicts, several minor skirmishes, and was the mainstay of the carrier attack force for almost 30 years. It had a remarkably short gestation period, and an even quicker retirement.

Some of the Intruder's history, particularly toward the end, is confusing. The Navy was in the middle of various major modifications to the A-6 when the decision was made to quickly remove the type from service to free up funding for the F/A-18E/F. Much of the documentation therefore reflected plans, not actuality. For instance, most lists of the aircraft which received the Boeing composite wing contained all the aircraft programmed to get the wing — not necessarily which ones actually did before the type was retired. Similarly, KA-6D conversion lists often contain aircraft scheduled for conversion, but which were scrapped in-place at the Grumman St. Augustine facility instead. Some aircraft were converted more than once (and, at least once, to the same configuration!), adding to the confusion. I have attempted to sort out what I could, but cannot verify the accuracy of some of the aircraft numbers.

This book only covers the A-6 and KA-6 — the EA-6 variants require a volume of their own, and will be addressed in the future.

ACKNOWLEDGMENTS

This book has been a long time in the making. It was commissioned by another publisher six years ago who later decided not to continue the project. Recently the publisher of the *WarbirdTech Series* decided that a few additional U.S. Navy aircraft were needed to round out the series. During this period, a great many people have contributed photos and information, including: Mick Roth; Robert F. Dorr; Tony Thornborough; Darryl Shaw; Vance Vasquez; LCDR Rick Morgan, USN (Ret); Robert L. Lawson; Jan Jacobs; Chris Reed; Brian J Plescia; Bryan Nylander; CDR Jeff Winston; Philip Friddell; MajGen William B. Fleming, USMC (Ret); Gil Murdock, Lockheed-Sanders; Lois Lovisolo, Grumman History Office; Tom Kane, Bob Hughes and William Morrissey, Grumman; Colonel Howard Wolf, USMC (Ret); and Dick Blenck. Special thanks also go to Jay Miller and my mother, Mary E. Jenkins.

A very plain-Jane A-6A (155658) from VA-42 shows the squat shape of the Intruder. (Grumman via the Robert F. Dorr Collection)

BUCKING THE TREND

THE BEGINNING OF ALL-WEATHER ATTACK

The American experience during the Korean conflict graphically demonstrated the need for tactical air in support of forces on the ground. Nevertheless, during the late 1940s and early 1950s, Naval Aviation seemed more intent on building its strategic forces with procurements of the North American AJ-1 (A-2A) Savage, a 50,000-pound medium bomber designed around a nominal 10,000-pound nuclear weapon, and the follow-on 70,000-pound Douglas A3D-1 (A-3A) Skywarrior, which was designed around the same requirement.

The ultimate statement of Cold War Naval Aviation was the North American A3J-1 (A-5A) Vigilante, a long-range supersonic bomber that would eventually find successful use as a long-range reconnaissance aircraft. By the late 1950s, however, the Navy's strategic focus shifted from airborne systems to its new ballistic missile submarines, mainly because it was becoming increasingly obvious that manned aircraft could no longer attack heavily defended strategic targets.

The Korean experience demonstrated that the Navy's, and the Air Force's for that matter, current aircraft were severely hampered in their ability to wage a "limited" war. The Navy jet fighters had speed, but lacked range, ordnance capacity, and sophisticated weapons delivery systems. The new strategic bombers could not carry any significant amount of conventional ordnance. The Douglas A4D-2 (A-4B) Skyhawk was still new and promising in the light attack role, but the primary tactical attack aircraft, the propeller-driven Douglas AD-6/7 (A-1H/J) Skyraider, was slow and rapidly becoming obsolete.

Nevertheless, it was the relative success of the A-1 during the Korean conflict that was in the minds of a Navy Long Range Objectives (LRO) study group as it drafted requirements for the next generation of Naval tactical attack aircraft in 1955. The LRO foresaw a potential increase in "limited" conflicts instead of the all-out nuclear war for which the United States was prepar-

The A2F-1 full-scale mockup shows the new stand-off weapons that the aircraft was initially intended to be armed with — the XASM-N-8 Corvus under the centerline and an AGM-N-7 Bullpup (later redesignated AGM-12) under the wing. Although the vertical stabilizer differs in detail, the overall shape of the A-6 is clearly evident in the mockup. (Grumman via Tony Thornborough)

The second A2F-1 (147865) at MCAS Cherry Point in October 1962. Note the intruder logo on the nose. The dark area on the bottom of the exhaust nozzles is the part that rotated downward to maximize the design's short-takeoff potential. Evaluation of the concept on the initial prototypes showed that the slight benefits were not worth the complexity of the installation and it was deleted from production aircraft. (Naval Historical Center)

ing. The group saw the need for a fast (but still subsonic) all-weather attack aircraft that would use an advanced conventional weapons delivery system. A short take-off and landing (STOL) version would be needed for the Marine Corps which required a versatile close air support (CAS) aircraft capable of providing accurate weapons delivery in any weather from relatively austere airfields near the front lines.

As a result of the LRO study, during the summer of 1956 the Navy and Marine Corps began to formulate Type Specification 149 for a common Navy attack and Marine CAS aircraft. On 2 October 1956, the Chief of Naval Operations issued an operational requirement (CA-01504) for the new aircraft, and on 5 March 1957 the Navy announced its intention to conduct a design competition.

The requirement would eventually specify a 500-knot, two-seat, medium-attack aircraft with an all-weather bombing system capable of delivering nuclear as well as conventional ordnance. The aircraft was also to use two new stand-off weapons — XASM-N-8 Corvus (later canceled) and AGM-N-7 Bullpup (later redesignated AGM-12). For the conventional attack role, the aircraft would need to carry two 1,000-pound bombs over a 300 nautical mile (nm) radius with a one hour loiter time over the target. The nuclear strike role was to use a 2,000-pound nuclear weapon on a 1,000 nm mission, but was strictly secondary since the Navy already had a large supply of nuclear bombers. The new carrier-based warplane was to operate from both the hydraulic catapults aboard the remaining *Essex*-class carriers and the steam catapults on the new *Forrestal*-class supercarriers.

Grumman Aircraft Engineering Corporation received the Request for Proposal in February 1957, and submitted a response on 16 August 1957. An engineering team under Lawrence (Larry) M. Mead and Robert Nafis began with a series of twin-engined bombers with M-shaped wings similar in appearance to the Ilyushin Il-28. The first of these designs was finalized on 27 February 1957 and a series of variations known as Designs 128M, 128M2, 128M3, and 123M4 were explored by Mead and his engineers. t did not take long for Mead and Nafis to discard the M-winged concept in favor of a more conventional swept-wing aircraft with two non-afterburning turbojet engines and side-by-side seating. On 12 March 1958, Grumman's Bill Cochran was named program manager for the new Design 128Q. Tragically, Cochran was killed two months later, and Bruce Tuttle subsequently replaced him.

Also competing were Bell, Boeing, McDonnell Douglas, Lockheed, Martin, North American, and Vought. Four of the manufacturers — Boeing, Douglas, Martin, and Vought — each hedged their bets and submitted two different designs, one powered by a turboprop engine, the other by a turbojet. Bell submitted a true VSTOL design that appeared to represent too much technical risk and was quickly rejected. The other three contenders each submitted fairly conventional designs powered by turbojet engines.

In December 1957 the list was narrowed to Douglas, Grumman, and Vought, and on 2 January 1958 the Navy announced that Grumman had won (Larry Mead apparently had been notified by phone on 30 December 1957, but the official announcement waited three days for paperwork to be completed). Grumman and the Navy entered final negotiations a week later.

On 14 February 1958, Grumman received a $3,410,148 preliminary development contract (No. 58-524c) for continued engineering design and to construct a mock-up of the A2F-1 Intruder. One of the major innovations proposed by Grumman was to consider the aircraft and all of its systems as a single entity instead of the usual approach of the primary contractor being responsible for the airframe, and other manufacturers being responsible for each of their individual systems (radar, engines, etc.), with the government ensuring they all worked together. For the Intruder, Grumman would be responsible for it all (it should be noted that a similar approach had been tried, fairly successfully, by the Air Force on the Convair F-102 Delta Dagger several years earlier).

The Grumman proposal team spent considerable time with operational attack crews attempting to determine the optimal design for the new attack aircraft, and much of what had been learned was incorporated into the final configuration. The company had explored many variations of its basic design before settling on the definitive 128Q model. The true mid-wing designs were too heavy, had too much drag, and were structurally complex. The low-wing designs made engine maintenance and removal difficult and limited the number and types of weapons that could be carried.

Excellent flying qualities in both the carrier and combat environment were a primary consideration for Larry Mead and his team. Moving the horizontal and vertical stabilizers as far aft as possible, while still fitting onto the 56-foot elevators on the *Essex*-class carriers, provided excellent stability. An efficient cruise capability at moderate mach numbers was needed to meet the long-range and loiter requirements, calling for a low-wetted area and quickly ruling out engine nacelles slung under the wings like those on the A-3. The requirements for relatively low carrier landing approach speeds dictated an efficient high lift system for the wing, initially consisting of leading edge slats and double-slotted flaps, along with wing spoilers for lateral control.

The 51-foot wingspan was larger than many designers would have chosen for fast flight at low altitudes, but it was the only solution to meeting the range and loiter requirements. Intruder crews therefore had a bumpier ride at low altitudes than the occupants of the comparable but smaller-winged and faster British Buccaneer. A similar fate awaited the much-later McDonnell Douglas F-15E Strike Eagle, which was adapted from a large-wing air-superiority fighter. Although uncomfortable at times for the crew, the mission was not compromised.

Aircraft carrier dimensions also dictated the location of the five weapons stations which had to fit within the 25.33-foot width limits that allowed two "folded" aircraft to pass each other through the fire doors of *Essex*-class carriers. Pylons could not be hung efficiently on the folding part of the wing since the

The fourth A2F-1 (147867) in December 1973. The fuselage speed brakes — shown fully extended — had perforations intended to prevent buffeting from affecting the tail surfaces. These speedbrakes were not considered effective and were later replaced by the split wingtip speedbrakes. (Ron McNiel via the Mick Roth Collection)

This A-6A (149940) from the second production batch was assigned to the Naval Air Test Center at Patuxtent River on 1 August 1974. (Ray leader via the Mick Roth Collection)

structure would have been unacceptably heavy, and loading and arming weapons on these pylons would have meant lowering the wings earlier than desired.

A single Mk 28 or Mk 43 nuclear weapon on the centerline and four 300-gallon external fuel tanks on the wings represented the nuclear strike configuration. For conventional missions, five 1,030-pound Mk 83 iron bombs or five racks with up to 30 Mk 81 Snakeyes could be loaded. A 15,939-pound load could be carried on a 2.9-hour mission on internal fuel alone, or up to 5.8 hours with in-flight refueling. The A2F-1 was also capable of carrying up to four Bullpup air-to-ground missiles, the Corvus antiradiation missile having been canceled by this time.

An early decision was made in favor of twin engines, with the 8,500-pounds-thrust (lbf) Pratt & Whitney J52-P-6 selected for its reliability and performance. Two engines improved safety margins and their forward location enabled efficiently short intakes. With the engines positioned forward it was also possible to get fairly short tailpipes that were angled slightly out and down so that the thrust vectors were very close to the center of gravity in both side and plan view. This made single engine trim requirements negligible and lessened differential power effects.

The Marine Corps STOL requirement (l,500-foot takeoff over a 50-foot obstacle from an 800-foot ground-roll with CAS warload) dictated either extraordinary high-lift performance or increased thrust. The Grumman solution was to provide "tilting tailpipes" for the J52 engines. By tilting the tailpipes 23 degrees down from their cruise position, the direct lift from the thrust reduced the estimated lift-off speed at Marine mission weight from 86 to 78 knots and the obstacle clearance distance by several hundred feet. To provide adequate low-speed pitch control with the pipes deflected down, Grumman provided geared elevators that came up as the leading edge of the horizontal stabilizer went up, but were locked out when the flaps were up. The tilting tailpipes were a major discriminator that contributed to Grumman winning the competition.

The heart of the new aircraft was DIANE (Digital Integrated Attack & Navigation Equipment), which significantly influenced the shape of the airframe from the beginning. DIANE (coincidentally, also the name of Bob Nafis' daughter) was built around an APQ-88 tracking radar, APQ-92 search radar, and ASN-31 inertial platform, integrated with an early ASQ-61 airborne digital computer. The limited capabilities of the available radars had driven the decision to use separate search and tracking units.

The cockpit display system was among the first to provide integrated data on a cathode ray tube (CRT). The pilot's analog flight director provided a synthetically generated directional and terrain clearance display from the phase-interferometer feature in the search radar. This was an early step that has led to modern highly-integrated multimode display systems.

The integration of sensors with the digital computer allowed Grumman to develop a breakthrough in weapons accuracy and flexibility in delivery modes, at least compared to previous analog fire control systems. Ballistic equations were solved with an RMS error of less than 0.3 mils over the entire operating range. Even when combined with sensor and other errors, the digital computer allowed the system to meet the specification requirement of 1.0 mils for free fall weapons. This came at a cost, however, and the complexity of DIANE is reflected by comparing the percentage costs for avionics among the aircraft's contemporaries: a mere 17 percent of the A-7A; 20

percent of the F-4B; and approximately 43 percent of the A-6A.

By the time construction of the mock-up began in September 1958, the aircraft configuration was well established. Changes introduced on the mock-up included modified canopy lines for improved visibility and less drag and a slightly larger vertical stabilizer. The trailing edge of the wing was straightened to eliminate the original mid-span break, allowing Grumman to replace the double-slotted flap with a simpler semi-fowler single-slotted tracked arrangement. Perhaps most significantly, Grumman adopted a nose wheel tow catapult system for the A2F-1. This added a small amount of additional weight but revolutionized catapulting forever.

Previously, carrier-borne aircraft were launched with a "bridle system" consisting of steel cables that connected the aircraft to the steam shuttle on the catapult. Several accidents had been caused by cables getting entangled with parts of the aircraft or weapons loads. The new nose wheel tow introduced several improvements, notably reduced time between aircraft launches and improved safety. It was originally designed for the Grumman E-2 Hawkeye and quickly adopted by Larry Mead for the A-6. The concept was first tested on a North American AJ-1 Savage, with the North American T-2 Buckeye the last bridle aircraft operated by the U.S. Navy. However, the French and Argentinean Navy still use the bridle system (although the Rafale will use nose wheel tow).

The construction of the Intruder airframe was highly conservative, employing an aluminum semi-monocoque fuselage combined with large sandwich or honeycomb access panels. The aircraft featured a deep keel manufactured from solid steel and titanium sheets to absorb the local stress and heat generated by the engines. The wing and empennage were of aluminum multibeam construction covered by machined skin and used conventional honeycomb-stiffened control surfaces. The wing consisted of a center section with port and starboard inner and outer panels. The entire center section of the wing, a continuous box-beam which passed through the fuselage, was milled from a single piece of aluminum alloy. The inner wing panels were bolted to a continuous box-beam which ran through the center-section, while the outer panels were joined at the wing-fold joint by four steel hinges. Wing-locking was achieved by hydraulically-driven pins.

Trailing-edge flaps extended across an unusually high percentage of the wing, eliminating the possibility of conventional ailerons. Lateral control was provided by spoilers on the upper wing surface that operated differentially for roll control in flight. These could also be used to "dump" lift once the aircraft had landed, thus increasing the load on the undercarriage and the effective-

One of the early A-6As (149484, redesignated NA-6A) was used as the prototype for the KA-6D modification. The aircraft is shown here at NATC Pax River on 20 March 1973. Note the refueling hose tube under the rear fuselage and the lack of a refueling probe ahead of the cockpit. (Stephen H. Miller via the Mick Roth Collection)

Another early A-6A (149486) on 20 October 1974 at the Naval Missile Center at Pt. Mugu, California. The air refueling probe ahead of the cockpit was initially intended to be removable, but all production aircraft had fixed units. (Stephen H. Miller via the Mick Roth Collection)

ness of the wheel brakes. The spoilers, however, did present some problems. Because they straddled the wing-fold area, the spoilers had to be neutral with the flaps retracted before the wings could be folded without damaging the spoilers. An innovative mechanical device prevented folding the wings unless they were in this configuration.

Accommodations were provided for a pilot and a bombardier/navigator (B/N) in a side-by-side arrangement. In a unique solution to the normal problem of sideways pilot visibility for side-by-side seating, Grumman placed the pilot slightly ahead and above the B/N, ensuring a decent field of vision.

Fully assembled, the A-6A's design load factor was +6.5g at 36,526 pounds, slightly less than contemporary naval fighters (which were usually rated to +7.5g). The main landing gear and arresting hook were designed to cope with a 20.3 feet per second trap at 33,637 pounds without permanent ill-effect on the aircraft. On later A-6s, the maximum catapult weight was increased to 58,600 pounds and the maximum trap weight was 36,000 pounds.

Then came an unusual embarrassment for an engineering company with Grumman's excellent reputation. A mistake in the cruise drag estimates occurred when the wrong reference wing area was used in calculating wind tunnel data. To correct the error, Grumman added two feet to the wing span (to 53 feet), improving its aspect ratio from 5.00 to 5.31, and finding room for an additional 1,000 pounds of fuel in the process. At the same time, the computer's memory was doubled, literally filling up the space in the cockpit between the B/N's legs (drum memory was bulky, not like current-day memory). Grumman also doubled the air conditioning capacity since heat rejection numbers for the advanced avionics began to exceed the original capacity.

Bruce Tuttle provided a progress report to the Navy on 3 February 1959 that indicated things were progressing well with the A2F-1. However, Grumman was already looking at another customer — the U.S. Air Force. Grumman Design 128B was a response to Air Force requirement SR-195 for a tactical strike/reconnaissance aircraft. It used the basic A2F-1 airframe with a ventral canoe fairing housing a reconnaissance pod with a high-capacity electrical generator, television viewer, APQ-55 side-looking radar, KA-5 cameras, and additional fuel. The primary armament was four Bullpup air-to-ground

---

[*] There is some doubt whether this designation applied to all eight aircraft. Some references state that it did, others indicate that only the first two aircraft carried the "Y" prefix. For the sake of separating them from the production aircraft, the "Y" is used here for all eight aircraft that functioned as prototypes.

10   WARBIRD**TECH**
         S E R I E S

missiles. For whatever reasons, the Air Force was not interested, and the design was not pursued.

On 26 March 1959 Grumman received a $101,701,000 "cost plus incentive fee" development contract, the first awarded by the Navy for the development of a major weapons system. Construction of eight YA2F-1 prototypes* began early in 1959, even before the Navy had reviewed the full scale mock-up. Only minor changes were found necessary when the mock-up was finally reviewed in September 1959.

The first prototype (BuNo 147864) was assembled at Plant 4 in Bethpage and conducted engine run-ups on the adjacent airfield. It was then partially disassembled and trucked to the Grumman facility at Calverton which offered a longer runway. On 19 April 1960 Grumman test pilot Bob Smyth took the Intruder on its first flight with the tilting tailpipes in the down position and the landing gear and flaps extended. The flight went smoothly, with no major anomalies. This aircraft was carrying only essential communications and navigation electronics, plus a large flight test instrumentation package. A month later, the Navy and Grumman held the formal roll-out ceremony at Calverton.

One of the early test objectives was to verify the performance of the tilting tailpipe concept. The pipes cranked up and down and vectored the thrust flawlessly, with the geared elevator handling all necessary trim changes. However, actual short-field performance was disappointing — landing speed was reduced by only eight knots at routine approach weights. The aircraft could land with the "pipes up" in a shorter distance than it could take off at heavy weights with the pipes pointing down. Furthermore, the Navy was content with the "pipes up" landing speed of 120 knots and, after considerable "lively debate" with the marines, the vectored thrust feature was deleted from the eighth aircraft (BuNo 148618) and all subsequent models. Interestingly, the concept would resurface on some advanced A-6F derivatives almost 30 years later.

The second and third prototypes were completed by September 1960 and commenced a detailed structural and aerodynamic flight test program, respectively. The flight test program generally proceeded smoothly, but not totally without incident. The second aircraft (BuNo 147865), which made its first flight on 18 July 1960 from Bethpage, had a controllable fuel shut-off valve between the two main tanks in the

The same early A-6A (149484) seen on page 9 as it appeared in November 1975 when the aircraft was assigned to the Naval Air Test Center. Most of the aircraft assigned to the various test series carried orange or red markings on the wingtips, vertical stabilizer, and around the air intakes. The wing fold mechanism was relatively straight-forward (at least when compared to other Grumman aircraft like the E-2 Hawkeye). (Dennis R. Jenkins)

fuselage so that the center of gravity could be varied during flight tests. Due to a nomenclature problem, this valve was closed instead of open during the first flight and the rear engine feed tank went dry, causing both engines to flame out just as the aircraft entered the downwind leg while landing at Calverton. Grumman test pilot Ernie Vonderheyden was able to dead stick the aircraft to a successful landing, demonstrating its flying qualities in the process.

Just before the first Navy Preliminary Evaluation (NPE-1) in October 1960, Vonderheyden was checking out high-g power-on maneuvers with the fuselage speedbrakes extended when he noticed sluggish pitch response. Grumman engineers found that the aerodynamic hinge moments on the horizontal stabilizer exceeded the capacity of the hydraulic actuator, which had stalled for a few seconds. The extended speedbrakes had changed the downwash pattern on the stabilizer and moved the center of pressure inboard and forward, increasing the hinge moments sharply. Grumman performed an extensive series of wind tunnel tests in January 1961 and three months later flew a redesigned stabilizer that was moved sixteen inches aft and had increased capacity actuators.

More changes came in May 1961 after NPE-1A. The A2F-1 initially was designed with conventional aft fuselage speedbrakes that had perforations intended to prevent buffeting from affecting the tail surfaces. The Navy determined that the fuselage speedbrakes were not sufficiently effective for either the dive bombing mission or for work around the carrier where instantaneous drag control was needed during landing. Considering potential buffeting, interference with external stores, and the possibility of large potential trim changes, it was decided that the best available location for additional braking surfaces was on the wingtips. Therefore, split wingtip speedbrakes became a standard feature of all production Intruders.

These split speedbrakes (which could open up to 120 degrees) were so successful that the fuselage speedbrakes on early aircraft were usually bolted closed and the actuators removed. In later aircraft the fuselage location was simply paneled over, although the unused speedbrake remained on all Intruders. Initial concerns about asynchronous operation of the wingtip units were overcome by interconnecting control cables and a hydraulic control valve, which was later replaced by a simple pressure tee to both wings.

Two additional changes were incorporated on the first production aircraft. The rudder chord was increased to provide better spin recovery characteristics and a fixed in-flight refueling probe was installed on the nose, replacing the detachable unit used on the initial prototypes.

The fourth prototype (BuNo 147867) was the first all-up avionics aircraft and made its maiden flight in early December 1960. However, since Grumman had not put the avionics together in a lab before the first flight, it took weeks before anything worked well enough to do much meaningful testing. The basic reliability of the electronic equipment was poor, the environmental testing had not been rigorous enough, and the lack of integration testing was disastrous. It provided a valuable lesson for Grumman and the Navy regarding the complexities of modern integrated aircraft systems. The fifth and seventh aircraft (BuNos 148615/148617) were delivered by September 1961 and performed navigation, weapons, and track radar tests.

In November 1961, the first Avionics NPE uncovered major deficiencies in the brightness and resolution of the cockpit displays. Also, the basic system reliability problems were still too serious to ignore. The first major Engineering Change Proposal (ECP) was approved in April 1962 intended mostly to upgrade the system reliability and the display quality. The pilot's horizontal display was changed to a 5-inch CRT and the navigator's 5-inch display enlarged to 7 inches. These changes resulted in delaying the first avionics Board of Inspection & Survey (BIS) tests and the start of fleet training by almost a year from the original schedule.

Nevertheless, the Intruder was quick to demonstrate its potential. In December 1961 LCDR "Bud" Ekas flew the seventh prototype A2F-1 from California to Virginia, unrefueled, in four hours three minutes. Another NATC A2F-1 later flew from Patuxent River to Paris, France, covering the 3,500-mile distance using five drop tanks without refueling.

On 18 September 1962, the A2F-1 became the A-6A under the Department of Defense's newly adopted uniform designation system. The airframe BIS also began in October 1962 and proceeded without incident. Then came sea-going trials aboard the USS *Enterprise* (CVAN-65) off the Virginia Capes, including maximum weight launches and traps. The A-6A rapidly acquired an excellent reputation for carrier suitability and performed well over 10,000 carrier landings before it had its first major landing accident aboard ship.

THE FIRST 2 INTRUDERS

1950s HIGH TECH

By late 1962 Grumman was building Intruders at a rate of two per month. Despite the avionics reliability problems, the aircraft was such a vast leap forward in range, payload, ordnance versatility, and all-weather attack capability that the Navy could not get them fast enough.

A-6A

The first step toward the introduction of the new attack aircraft into the fleet was the formation of a training squadron, known at the time as a replacement air group (RAG) and today as a fleet replenishment squadron. The East Coast Intruder RAG was VA-42 at NAS Oceana, Virginia.

On 1 February 1963 Vice Admiral Frank O'Breirne, Commander of U.S. Forces Atlantic, took formal delivery of the first two A-6As and issued them to VA-42. The squadron immediately began Intruder training, a mission it was still performing three decades later when the Intruder was retired. It was a rough beginning. In the early 1960s, the Navy had almost no active-duty experience with second crew members in its fighters or attack aircraft. VA-42 had difficulty training bombardier/navigators in Douglas TA-3B Skywarriors with aging and nonrepresentative ASB-7 radar. There was an urgent need for a dedicated A-6 systems training aircraft, but the TC-4C Academe would not be introduced until much later. Many of the early Intruders were delivered without some or all of the complex DIANE system. On those aircraft that did have it, the DIANE did not work well — if at all. Still, the aircraft were adequate to begin initial training, which proceeded at a rapid pace.

With the United States becoming increasingly involved in Southeast Asia, fielding the new medium-attack aircraft took on greater urgency. The first fleet squadrons to receive the Intruder were VA-75 and VA-85. The squadrons came up to strength quickly and were deployed to Southeast Asia where combat sorties against North Vietnam began on 1 July 1965. Early strikes were carried out against key highway bridges at Bac Bang and other targets south of Hanoi. A month later, a pair of A-6As began dropping bombs on the Thanh Hoa powerplant south of Hanoi. DIANE worked some of the time, and the A-6A quickly became the only American warplane capable of operating deep inside North Vietnam at night — a source of some embarrassment to the U.S. Air Force. Still, VA-85 lost a total of six Intruders on this cruise.

Although the source of many headaches and highly demanding in terms of maintenance, the A-6's avionics were among the most advanced yet developed for a tactical aircraft. DIANE was composed of 10 principal items of equipment that allowed the crew to attack targets in any kind of weather without ever having to look out through the windscreen. Numerous weapons could be employed, with DIANE automatically computing the appropriate flight trajectory and release point for each.

The Naval Avionics Facility Indianapolis (NAFI) APQ-88 Ku-band tracking radar tracked moving targets on the ground that were designated by the azimuth and elevation crosshairs on the B/N's radarscope. The radar provided target elevation and range data to the navigation and

Although it looks like it should be an early prototype, this is actually the 26th A-6A (149940) assigned to the Naval Air Test Center. Note the long flight test instrumentation boom protruding from the nose. (Naval Historical Center)

GRUMMAN
A-6 INTRUDER

13

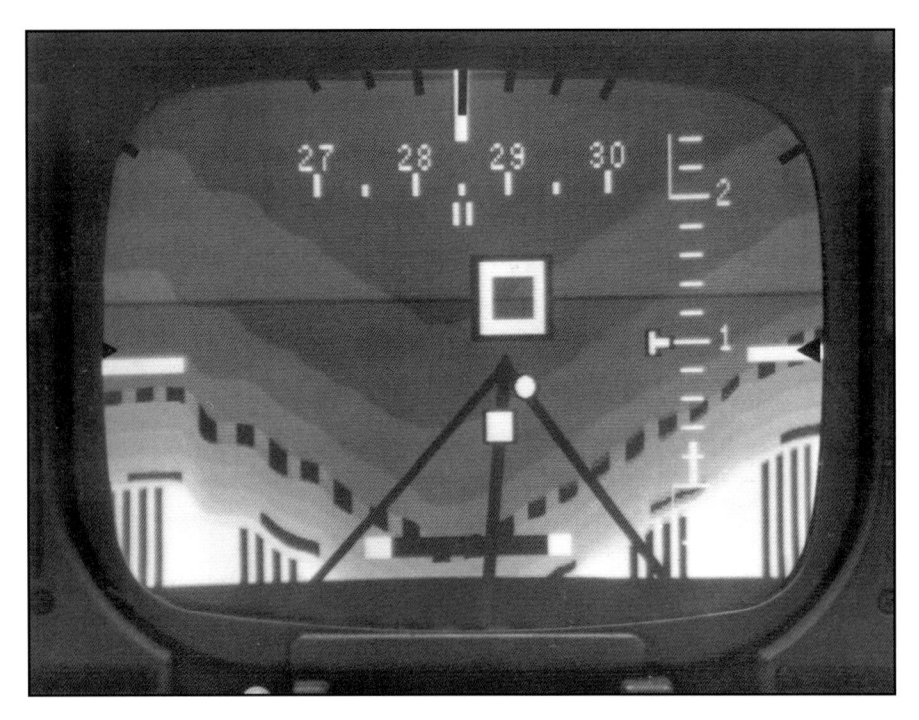

The Kaiser AVA-1 video display indicator (VDI) was a gray-green display that presented a graphical view of the world outside the cockpit. This was one of the first attempts to integrate multiple flight data onto a single display. (Kaiser Electronics via Tony Thornborough)

ballistics computers and also provided terrain-following data in the vertical axis on the E-scan displayed on the pilot's CRT. The pilot used this data in conjunction with the radar altimeter and vertical display indicator (VDI) to ensure that he did not fly the A-6A into "rock-infested clouds," as the Grumman flight manual put it. It is worth remembering that DIANE did not perform terrain following, but that the pilot manually flew the aircraft over obstacles based on cues provided on his CRT. A significantly more reliable version of this radar, the Norden APQ-112, was installed in the 60th and all subsequent A-6As, and retrofitted to most earlier aircraft.

The Norden APQ-92 Ku-band search radar was used to detect moving and stationary ground targets, the former via the airborne moving target indicator feature. It also provided search radar terrain clearance data on the VDI, represented by a 53 degree by 26 degree window of the terrain around the aircraft's armament datum line, to assist the pilot in navigating to the target.

The Litton ASN-31 inertial navigation system (INS) provided aircraft attitude, horizontal and vertical velocity, and heading based on data derived from accelerometers mounted on a gyro-stabilized platform.

The Sperry ASW-16 automatic flight control system (AFCS) was a three-axis autopilot that could be coupled to the computer and navigation equipment to provide "hands off" flight to the target area. Flight stability was performed automatically by using the trim actuators. Basic altitude, attitude, and mach number hold modes were also available. Even with the autopilot engaged the pilot could pull and push the aircraft up and down over obstacles en route as necessary for terrain following.

Based on inputs from the INS and radar altimeter, the CP-729/A air data computer supplied altitude, static pressure, mach number, and airspeed data to the AFCS, VDI, and ballistics computer, together with the flight instruments. Later A-6As used upgraded CP-863/A or CP-864/A air data computers.

The Litton ASQ-61 ballistics computer used inputs from the INS, air data computer, and both radars to calculate the optimum automatic weapons release point during attack profiles. It used a complex series of preprogrammed ballistics equations that correlated aircraft altitude, target height, the assumed dive and pull-up forces, and the characteristics of the weapon employed. This early digital computer used drum memory as its primary storage device. Later A-6As used a slightly upgraded ASQ-61A unit.

The Kaiser AVA-1 video display indicator (VDI) was a gray-green display that presented a graphical account of the world outside the cockpit. It displayed radar-derived terrain information and also provided comprehensive steering and attack information in all modes using heading lines and cues for target position, commit, and pull-up. The positions of two targets or waypoints could be inserted into DIANE and recalled to provide steering cues to the target. When operating against a target of opportunity, the B/N's radar crosshairs could be used to provide target azimuth on the VDI.

The APN-153 Doppler radar navigation set included a four-beam array under the aircraft that supplied ground speed and drift angle to the navigation computer to calculate the aircraft's ground track.

The APN-141 radar altimeter complemented the APN-153 by providing a continuous display of aircraft height up to 5,000 feet, used primarily to assist during landing approaches and to provide height display during dive-bombing runs.

The AIC-14 integrated communications, navigation, and identification system kept the crew in touch with the outside world, and with navigation aids such as TACAN (tactical air navigation) and ADF (automatic direction finder). It also provided standard military IFF (identification friend or foe) and civilian ATC (air traffic control) transponder functions.

DIANE allowed the aircraft to place ordnance on the target day or night in all but the worst weather. With the B/N's direct view radarscope indicator (DVRI) crosshairs on the desired target, the tracking radar would provide target elevation data to calculate the automatic weapons release point while the VDI supplied the pilot with steering instructions. Because not all targets were radar-significant, and the DVRI imagery was fuzzy at best, the B/N frequently had the crosshairs positioned over a prominent nearby landmark or beacon referred to as an offset aim point (OAP). With the OAP's range and bearing to the true target entered into the system — including any difference in ground elevation between the two points — DIANE would compare the relative positions of target and OAP and provide steering instructions to the pilot while computing the automatic weapons release point.

Several "blind" attack profiles were available. STRAIGHT PATH was an unaccelerated level flight, dive, or climb maneuver onto the target. ROCKET entailed a straightforward dive and pull-out; GENERAL was highly flexible in that DIANE provided solutions for all ballistic shapes (i.e., conical low-drag or Snakeye high-drag bombs) except rockets, and which typically called for an accelerated dive and 4-g pull-up dive toss maneuver to lob the weapons onto the target. The last profile was HIGH LOFT, a traditional half-Cuban eight pull-up maneuver with weapons release occurring at 70 to 85 degrees in order to lob ordnance onto the target while permitting a rapid, safe egress from severe blasts such as those generated by tactical nuclear weapons.

The need for modifications to both radar units became evident during the initial A-6A Southeast Asia deployment. One major complaint was the system's marginal capability in tracking small moving targets such as truck convoys. Although still troubled by maintenance and reliability problems with DIANE, the initial nine aircraft of VA-85 averaged 12 sorties per day during their early Vietnam use. The daily usage of individual aircraft averaged between 1.2 and 1.4 sorties per aircraft per day. With less than 20 percent of the total number of aircraft on board USS *Kitty Hawk*, the A-6As were delivering approximately 50 percent of the carrier's bomb load over North Vietnam during the monsoon season.

Overall systems availability of the A-6As for the first two deployed squadrons averaged only 35 percent when the aircraft first began operating over North Vietnam in the summer of 1965. By late 1966 this had improved to almost 70 percent after various modifications had been incorporated and maintenance personnel became more proficient. The

An obviously staged photo showing the weapons available to the A-6 during 1966. In addition to the typical array of conventional "iron bombs" there are five Bullpup air-to-ground missiles (to the right), four Sidewinder air-to-air missiles (to the left), a buddy refueling pack, plus four weapons marked "secret" (in front of the aircraft). (U.S. Navy via Tony Thornborough)

An A-6A (152907) from VA-165 is catapulted from the USS Ranger in the Gulf of Tonkin during January 1968. The aircraft carries a load of Mk 82 500-pound bombs destined for a target in North Vietnam. (Naval Historical Center)

ordnance delivery accuracy of the A-6A also improved dramatically, and after the first year A-6A crews were allowed to engage targets without visually acquiring them. Maintenance requirements were very high, however, at approximately 90 maintenance man-hours per flight hour (MMH/FH).

These early A-6A operations brought to light some unexpected problems. It was found that some of the early maps of North Vietnam contained errors as great as three to four miles. As a consequence, the Navy began an extensive aerial mapping survey of North Vietnam with RA-5C Vigilante reconnaissance aircraft. During tests to determine the accuracy of the RA-5C, an oblique photograph of a California football field was taken from 60 miles away. When the photograph was scaled-out, the length of the playing field appeared as 100.1 yards, a discrepancy of only 0.1 yard. After several months, new, more accurate maps were made available to the attack crews and planners. This greatly improved the effectiveness of most strike missions, particularly those using OAPs.

The need to further improve the reliability of DIANE resulted in the System Improvement Program (SIP) beginning in the summer of 1966. The APQ-88 tracking radar was substantially redesigned by Norden Systems and redesignated APQ-112. Improved reliability was the primary goal of the redesign, although slightly improved resolution was also achieved. The APQ-88 had originally been designed only to track moving targets, but as it was being used extensively against fixed targets, the APQ-112 included specific provisions to track stationary targets.

The new radar used an internal Klystron tube as a substitute for an external microwave source to reduce corrosion. It also received various circuit improvements, modifications to correct an amplitude jitter effect, and a previous drift tendency in the

The A-6A assembly line at Grumman during 1967. Note the amount of plumbing and wiring running along the top of the fuselage behind the cockpit. (Grumman via Tony Thornborough)

unit was corrected by switching to a regulated voltage supply. The laminate skin of the original black radome was susceptible to fraying, a condition largely corrected by using a new neoprene overcoat which was generally a lighter color and was less susceptible to corrosion.

The SIP for the APQ-92 search radar included the use of new crystals to obtain greater reliability, and improvements in the stability of circuits to cut the drift rate. It also received the same Klystron fix as the tracking radar. The changes were not considered significant enough to merit a new designation.

DIANE represented the first major use of a programmable digital computer in an airborne weapons system. The P-1 through P-7B software, sequentially released throughout the 1960s, gradually brought about a series of minor performance improvements. By the end of the decade this included the ability to allow the search radar to perform some of the tracking radar's functions, thus paving the way for a single radar to take over both search and tracking tasks in the A-6E. The final release, the P-8 program, was introduced in early 1970 and included some major innovations. Most were intended to ease crew workload or to improve strike accuracy, but a new automatic AGM-45 Shrike missile delivery option was also included.

Although not integrated with DIANE, the defensive electronic countermeasures suite the A-6A entered service with was also an advanced system consisting of two AEL ALR-15 radar warning receivers, a Sanders ALQ-41 active countermeasures set, Sanders Associates ALQ-51 countermeasures set, and a Tracor ALE-18 chaff dispenser.

Before the advent of the KA-6D, standard A-6As equipped with a D-704 buddy refueling pod on the centerline were used as tankers. This Intruder is preparing to launch from the USS Constellation *in late 1968 with a buddy pod and four underwing fuel tanks.* (Naval Historical Center)

The two ALR-15 receivers were designed to detect enemy antiaircraft artillery (AAA) and surface-to-air missile (SAM) tracking radars, but proved nearly worthless in operation. The ALR-15 sets were soon replaced by a single Applied Technology Incorporated (ATI) APR-25 radar homing and warning (RHAW) receiver and a Magnavox APR-27 missile launch warning receiver.

The ALQ-41 was upgraded several times. Airframe Change (AFC) 123 replaced the ALQ-41 on the A-6A with the Sanders ALQ-100 on 15 April 1968. The ALQ-100 added long-armed spoon antennas that protruded from the inner wing pylons. Eventually the Sanders ALQ-126 replaced the ALQ-100, and the ALE-29 chaff dispenser replaced the ALE-18. Beginning in 1978 the

An A-6A from VA-75 — the first operational A-6 squadron — at DaNang, Vietnam. (Grumman via Tony Thornborough)

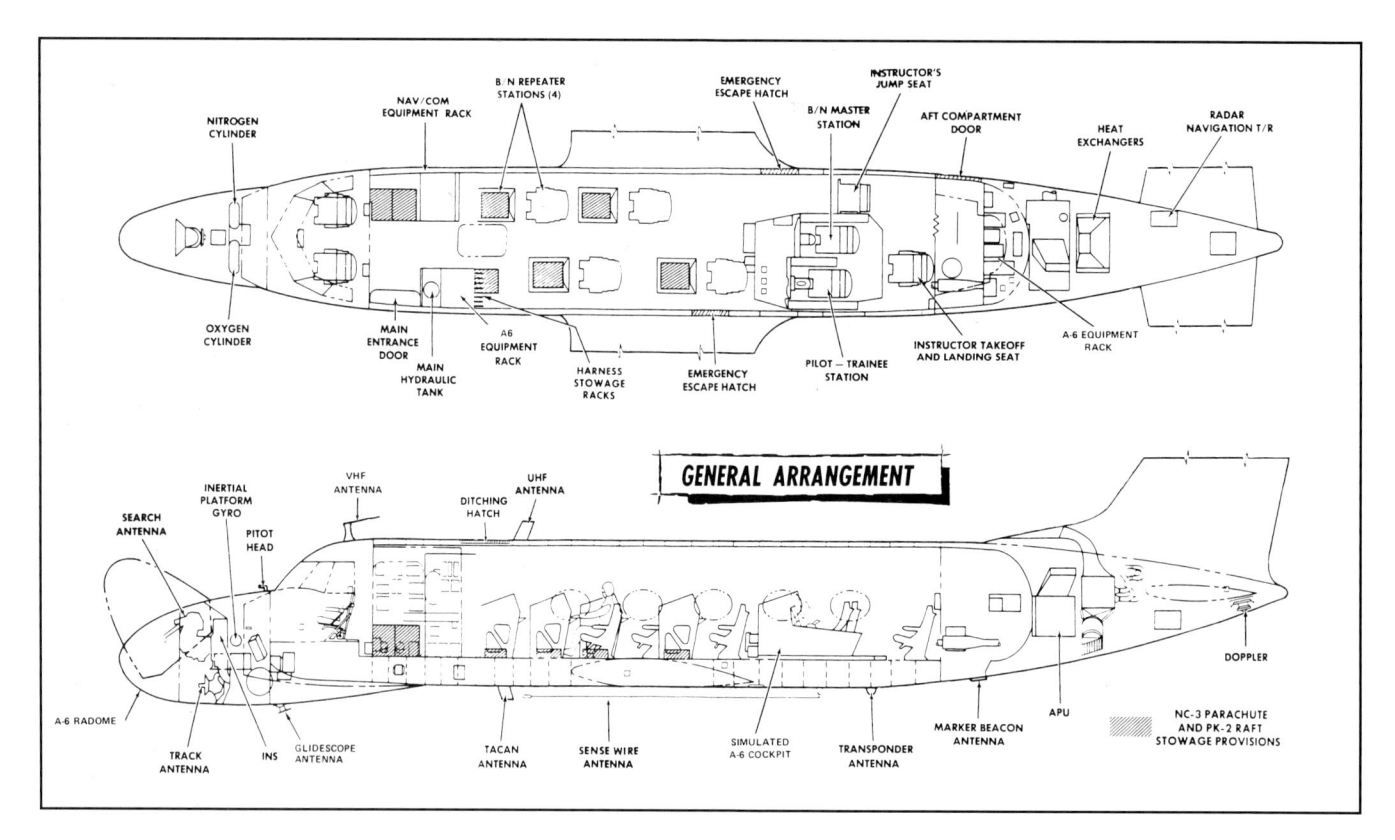

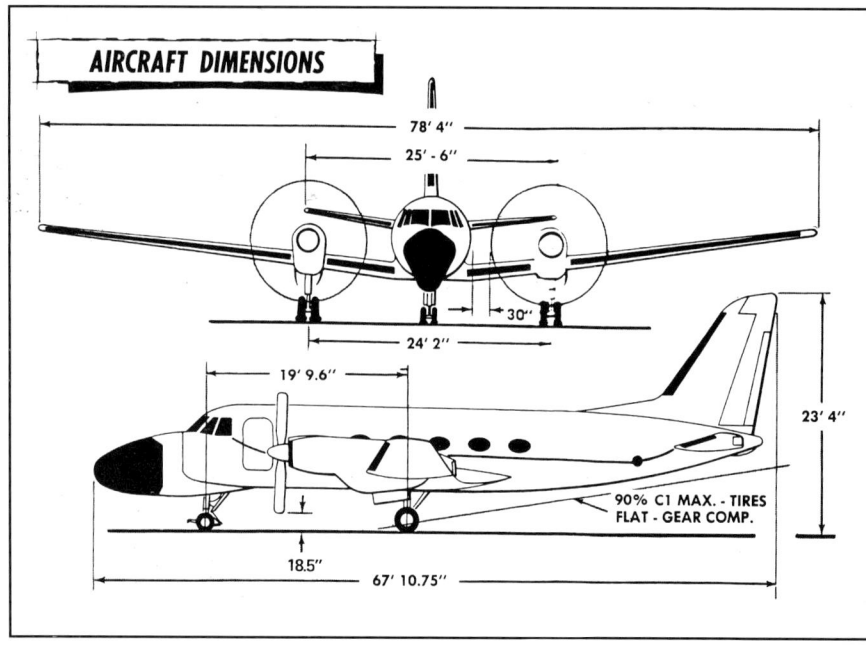

The general and interior arrangements of the TC-4C from the NATOPS manual. Note that a complete set of A-6 radars and avionics reside in the nose grafted onto the commercial Grumman G-159 Gulfstream I turboprop corporate aircraft. (U.S. Navy)

ALE-39 was introduced on A-6E aircraft that included an improved controller but continued to use the original ALE-29 dispensers.

As the Intruder became the fleet's standard medium-attack aircraft and the A-1 Skyraider retired to the boneyard, the Navy and Marine Corps continued to develop a comprehensive training syllabus for Intruder crews. Since there was no dedicated A-6 trainer, the courses were limited to classroom work and limited time in an A-6A with an instructor pilot. However, since there were only two seats, it was necessary for the pilot to attempt to instruct the student B/N, all the while still flying the aircraft. This was not a truly workable concept. A solution was found when Grumman G-159 Gulfstream I aircraft were fitted with a complete A-6 forward fuselage grafted on the nose — including a complete DIANE system — providing an extremely realistic trainer. The first TC-4C Academe (BuNo 155722) made its maiden flight at Calverton on 14 June 1967. Instructors and systems operators sat in the main fuselage to operate the simulators and evaluate the students.

A total of 9 TC-4Cs (BuNos 155722 through 155730) were delivered to the Navy during the late 1960s and eventually served with three training squadrons. Five years after

VA-42 became the East Coast A-6 training unit, a cadre from VAH-123 (an A-3 Skywarrior RAG that briefly possessed a few A-6As) formed the West Coast training squadron — VA-128 — on 1 September 1967. The Marine Corps also operated a training unit, VMAT(AW)-202, at MCAS Cherry Point, North Carolina, beginning 15 January 1968. The A-6A and TC-4C combination proved effective in training A-6 crews, eliminating the need for a proposed three-seat TA-6A trainer. The TC-4Cs were updated with A-6E target recognition attack multisensor (TRAM) avionics from 1978 through 1980.

The marines began deploying A-6As to Vietnam in December 1967 and flew combat missions from Da Nang and Chu Lai in South Vietnam and Nam Phong, Thailand. One unit, VMA(AW)-224, flew strikes from the USS *Coral Sea* (CVA-43) as part of Carrier Air Wing 15, as well as participating in the successful mining of Haiphong harbor in 1972.

Interestingly, the first three A-6As lost over Vietnam were destroyed by premature detonations of their own bombs. During 1965 the Intruder's wing stations were equipped with multiple bomb racks (MBRs) and carried World War II vintage bombs with mechanical nose fuses. When the aircraft released its bomb load in a relatively-steep dive, the fuse became armed approximately 0.7 seconds after release while the bomb was still directly underneath the aircraft. Because the MBR was not an ejection rack, the bombs in these three accidents tumbled into each other just under the aircraft and detonated, destroying the A-6s.

When it discovered the reason for the losses, the Navy restricted A-6s to straight-and-level bomb drops

A TC-4C (155722) from VA-128 visiting Buckley ANGB in Colorado on 28 June 1975. Normal ingress/egress was accomplished via the built-in airstairs, a feature retained from the Gulfstream I business aircraft. (Jack R. Bol via the Mick Roth Collection)

The markings on the Academe largely mimicked the markings used on the A-6s assigned to the same squadron. This TC-4C (155729) from VA-42 was photographed at NAS Oceana on 17 June 1975. (Mick Roth Collection)

Another TC-4C (155726) from VA-128 photographed in October 1974. The A-6 radome significantly degraded the forward visibility for the pilot, but overall the aircraft proved remarkably successful in its training role. (Mick Roth Collection)

GRUMMAN
A-6 INTRUDER

The A-6 was ungainly from almost any angle. Note the number of protuberances on the upper wing surface — two fences, a hinge cover, and two streamlined actuator/hinge covers for the wingtip speed brakes on each side. Despite its appearance, the aircraft proved to be rugged and very successful at its primary strike mission. (Mick Roth Collection)

until they could be retrofitted with the more advanced Douglas multiple ejector racks (MERs) and triple ejector racks (TERs). Both the MER and TER used pyrotechnic cartridges to kick the bombs away from the rack (and each other), virtually eliminating the possibility of the weapons bumping into one another anywhere near the aircraft.

Based on experience from Korea, in September 1958 the Naval Ordnance Test Station at China Lake began development of the AGM-45 Shrike anti-radar missile (ARM). Originally intended to counter AAA and early warning radars, Shrike would become the first operational antiradiation missile in the U.S. inventory during early 1965 and went on to form the basis for dedicated IRON HAND radar-killing missions.

Shrike used a Texas Instruments passive seeker to acquire and lock onto enemy radars at ranges of up to 40 miles. Because of their all-weather attack capabilities, the A-6As were a natural platform for the Shrike, a typical load comprising either two or four missiles. The early Shrike delivery modes required the aircraft be pointed in the direction of the target to allow the missile's seeker to acquire the radar, something that would remain true for azimuth even with the introduction of newer seekers. After launching a missile the aircraft would break away and the Shrike would home in on the electromagnetic radiation emitted by the target radar. At least that was the theory. Early operations using Shrike in Vietnam were generally unsuccessful, although improvements in tactics as well as modifications to the missile's seeker improved things somewhat.

The AGM-45 also enabled the crew to detect and attack enemy radars with conventional ordnance. The definitive P-8 computer program "Shrike ranging mode" made use of the Shrike's ability to detect emitters at ranges of up to 40 miles and relay that information to DIANE, which provided relevant target steering information on the VDI. To use this feature, the pilot flew the A-6A until the steering symbol was centered in the VDI, then pressed the COMMIT button to the first detent to input a single point azimuth reading. Then the pilot commenced a slow turn away from the emitter until the Intruder was at a relative bearing of 20 to 30 degrees in either direction, holding the aircraft steady until the IN RANGE cue started flashing. At this point the A-6A had flown far enough to permit a second azimuth reading to be taken, which the pilot accomplished by turning the A-6A back toward the target, centering the steering symbol in the VDI once more, and pressing the COMMIT button again.

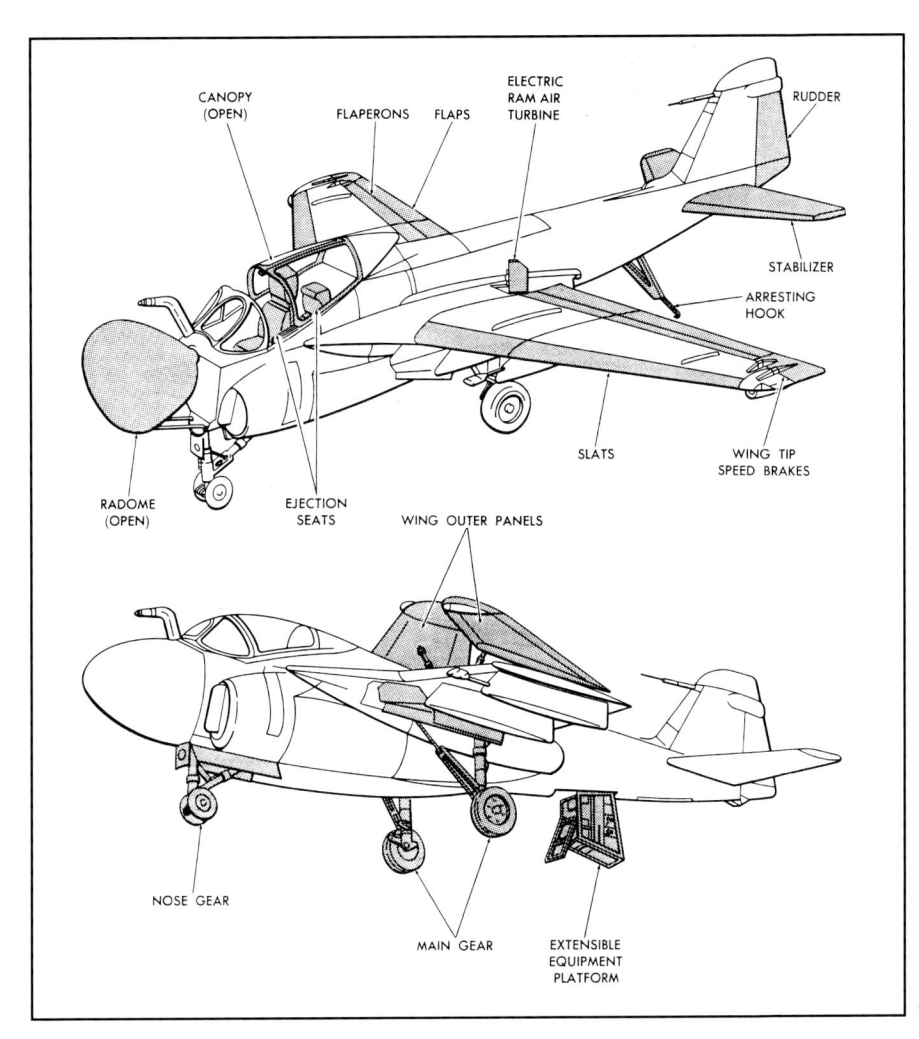

A diagram (left) from a service manual showing the major movable surfaces on the A-6A. The general arrangement diagram (below) shows the location of major components inside the aircraft. Note the extensible "bird cage" that held most of the DIANE components. (U.S. Navy)

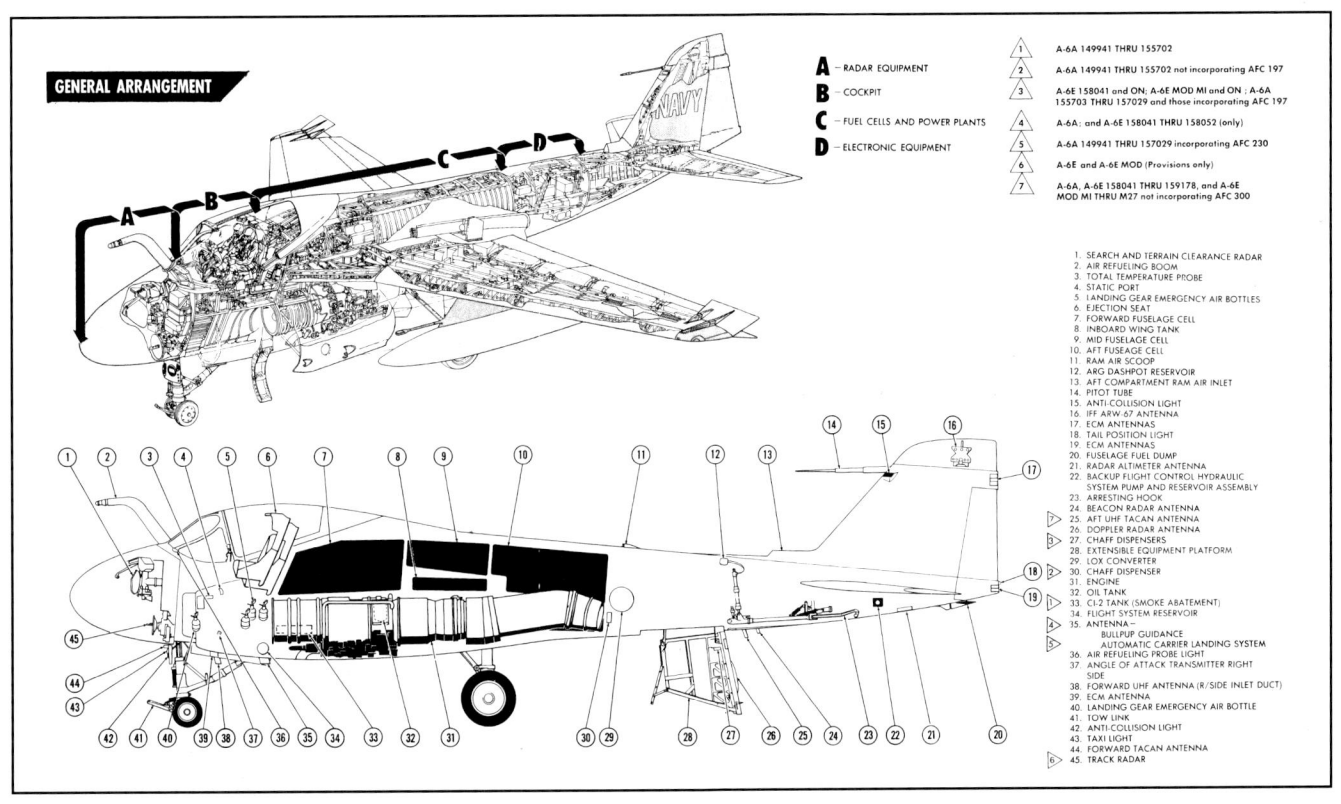

GRUMMAN A-6 INTRUDER

STORES	LOADING	STATION	SUSPENSION
BOMBS	1 2 3 4 5	1 2 3 4 5	
MK-81 LDGP (Conical Tails)	(See Note 1) ▽ ▽ ▽ ▽ ▽ ▽	(See Note 2) 1 1 1 1 3 2 3 2 3 6 5 6 5 6 6 6 6 6 6	AERO-7A A/A37B-5, TER A/A37B-6, MER A/A37B-1, MBR
MK-81 LDGP (Snakeye Tails)	▽ ▽ ▽ ▽ ▽ ▽	1 1 1 1 3 2 3 2 3 6 5 6 5 6 6 6 6 6 6	AERO-7A A/A37B-5, TER A/A37B-6, MER A/A37B-1, MBR
MK-82 LDGP (Conical Tails)	▽ ▽ ▽ ▽ ▽ ▽	1 1 1 1 3 2 3 2 3 6 5 6 5 6 6 6 6 6 6	AERO-7A A/A37B-5, TER A/A37B-6, MER A/A37B-1, MBR
MK-82 LDGP (Snakeye Tails)	▽ ▽ ▽ ▽ ▽ ▽	1 1 1 1 3 2 3 2 3 6 5 6 5 6 6 6 6 6 6	AERO-7A A/A37B-5, TER A/A37B-6, MER A/A37B-1, MBR
MK-83 LDGP	▽ ▽	1 1 1 1 3 2 3 2 3	AERO-7A A/A37B-5, TER
MK-84 LDGP		1 1 1 1 1	AERO-7A
AN-M81 Frag. AN-M88 Frag. (Conical Tails)		1 1 1 1 3 3 3 3 3 6 6 6 6 6	AERO-7A A/A37B-5, TER A/A37B-6, MER A/A37B-1, MBR
AN-M 57 A1 GP (Conical Tails)	▽ ▽ ▽ ▽	1 1 1 1 3 2 3 2 3 6 5 6 5 6	AERO-7A A/A37B-5, TER A/A37B-6, MER A/A37B-1, MBR
AN-M 64 A1 GP AN-M 65 A1 GP AN-M 66 A2 GP (Conical Tails)		1 1 1 1 1	AERO-7A
MK-94 Chemical		1 1 1 1 1 6 6 6 6 6	AERO-7A A/A37B-1, MBR
MK-77 Mod. 1, 2 Fire	▽ ▽ ▽ ▽ ▽ ▽ ▽ ▽	1 1 1 1 1 1 1 1 2 2 2 2	AERO-7A A/A37B-5, TER A/A37B-6, MER
MK-79 Mod. 1 Fire		1 1 1 1 1	AERO-7A
CBU-1A/A, CBU-2A CBU-2A/A	▽ ▽ ▽	1 1	A/A37B-6, MER
AN-M 64 A1 GP AN-M 65 A1 GP AN-M 66 A2 GP (Box Fins)		1 1 1 1 1	AERO-7A-1

STORES	LOADING	STATION	SUSPENSION
MISSILES AND ROCKET LAUNCHERS	1 2 3 4 5	1 2 3 4 5	
AGM-12B Bullpup "A"		1 1 1 1	AERO 5A-1
AGM-12C Bullpup "B"		1 1 1 1	AERO-7A
AGM-45A Shrike		1 1 1 1	AERO 5A-1
AIM-9B Sidewinder 1A or AIM-9D Sidewinder 1C		1 1 1 1	LAU-7A Launcher
LAU-32A/A LAU-32B/A LAU-3A/A	▽ ▽ ▽ ▽ ▽ ▽ ▽ ▽	1 1 1 1 3 2 2 3 3 2 2 3	AERO-7A A/A37B-5, TER A/A37B-6, MER
LAU-10/A		1 1 1 1	AERO-7A
TANKS AND PODS 300 gal. fuel tank		1 1 1 1 1	AERO-7A
D-704 Refueling Store (Buddy Tank)		1	AERO-7A

STORES	LOADING	STATION	SUSPENSION
MINES	1 2 3 4 5	1 2 3 4 5	
MK-36 Mine (MK-13 lug) MK-37 Parapack MK-27 Parapack		1 1 1 1 1	AERO-7A
MK-50 Mine MK-15 Parapack MK-38 Parapack		1 1 1 1 1 1 1	AERO-7A
MK-52 Mine MK-20 or MK-35 Parapack		1 1 1 1 1	AERO-7A

STORES	LOADING	STATION	SUSPENSION
TRAINING AND PYROTECHNICS	1 2 3 4 5	1 2 3 4 5	
MK-86 and MK-87, WSF	▽ ▽ ▽ ▽ ▽ ▽ ▽ ▽ ▽ ▽	1 1 1 1 3 2 3 2 3 6 5 6 5 6 2 2 2 2 2	AERO-7A A/A37B-5, TER A/A37B-6, MER A/A37B-1, MBR
MK-88 WSF		1 1 1 1 1	AERO-7A
MK-76 Mod. 4, 5PB		6 6 6	A/A37B-3, PMBR
MK-76 Mod. 5PB MK-14 Lug.		6 6 6 6 6	A/A37B-1, MBR
MK-89 PB MK-106 Mod. 3PB, 4PB		6 6 6	A/A37B-3, PMBR
AERO 6A, 6A-1, 6A-2		1 1 1 1	AERO-7A
AERO 7D	▽ ▽ ▽ ▽ ▽ ▽	1 1 1 1 3 2 2 3 3 2 2 3	AERO-7A A/A37B-5, TER A/A37B-6, MER
MK-6 Mod. 6 Parachute Flare		6 6 6 6 6 6 6 6 6 6 3 3 3 3 3 6 6 6 6 6 6 6 6 6 6 6 6 6 6 6	A/A37B-1, MBR A/A37B-3, PMBR A/A37B-5, TER A/A37B-6, MER A/A37B-1, MBR A/A37B-3, PMBR
AERO 8A-1 PBC (MK-76, MK-106)		1 1 1	AERO-7A

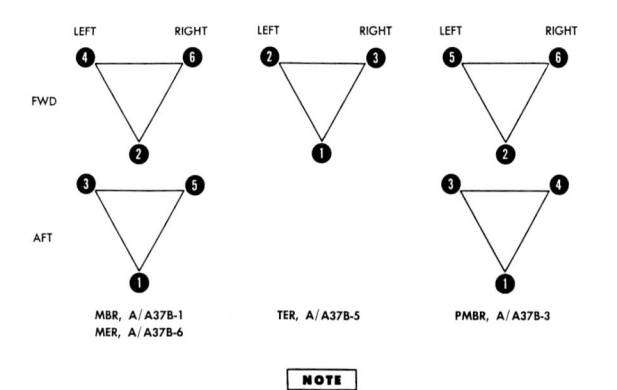

NOTE

1. WHERE LESS THAN THE MAXIMUM NUMBER OF STORES IS AUTHORIZED FOR CARRIAGE, A SCHEMATIC LOADING DIAGRAM IS PROVIDED. THE RACK STATION NUMBERS ARE SHOWN ABOVE. THE MAXIMUM ASYMMETRICAL (FORE AND AFT) LOADING PERMITTED ON THE MBR IS A 500 POUND CLASS STORE. MIXED LOADING OF DIFFERENT STORES ON THE SAME MULTIPLE RACK IS NOT PERMITTED EXCEPT FOR CBU.
2. THE NUMBERS LISTED IN THE STATION COLUMN DENOTE THE MAXIMUM NUMBER OF APPLICABLE STORES WHICH MAY BE CARRIED ON THE INDICATED RACK.

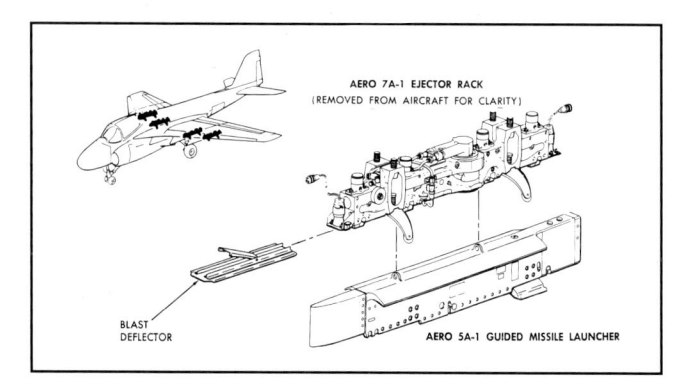

The weapons loading chart from the A-6A Conventional Weapons Loading Manual. The "LDGP" bombs are low-drag general-purpose iron bombs. Note that AIM-9 Sidewinders could be carried on all four wing pylons. Up to five 300-gallon drop tanks could be carried (one on each station). Before the advent of the KA-6D tanker, it was not unusual for an A-6A to carry a single D-704 buddy refueling pod on the centerline and a 300-gallon tank on each wing station — this configuration provided a decent indigenous tanking capability for the aircraft carriers. (U.S. Navy)

DIANE used the two azimuth readings to triangulate the enemy radar's position, which was then displayed on the B/N's radar scope. Thus it was possible to use Shrike as both a pure weapon and a target detection system. In the latter mode the use of steel pellet-filled CBUs ensured the radar suffered significant damage even if the bombs missed by 100 feet or so.

Several variants of the seeker were available to cover the different operating frequencies of the Soviet-supplied SA-2 and AAA guidance radars and the choice of seekers had to be made before the aircraft was launched on the mission. The Dash 1 and later Dash 3 seekers covered both AAA and the SA-2 operating frequencies; the Dash 3A and Dash 3B seekers were more selective and tailored to specific threats. The Shrike also had a limited range, which meant that crews had to bring their aircraft well within the lethal zone of the SA-2 in order to engage the Soviet weapon. Furthermore, if the enemy emitter stopped transmitting, Shrike would lose track of its target and plunge into the ground. This happened frequently when the North Vietnamese became wise to the presence of the IRON HAND aircraft and put radars on "dummy load," a standby status which inhibited transmissions. It has been estimated that the Shrike had an overall kill rate well under 15 percent during Vietnam operations.

Grumman completed the 480 unit production run (not including the eight prototypes) of A-6As in December 1970 with the last 223 aircraft equipped with improved 9,300-lbf J52-P-8A engines. Most surviving A-6As would be modified to either the KA-6D or A-6E configuration.

An early production A-6A (149482) assigned to the Pacific Missile Test Range (PMTC) during January 1976. Grumman had designed the A-6 to be easily serviceable with a minimum of workstands or special equipment — years before this became a trend among weapons designers. Installing most of the DIANE components in the bird cage was one of the innovations introduced on the A-6A that would continue on all subsequent models. (Mick Roth Collection)

An A-6A (155689) from VMA(AW)-533 approaching NAF Atsugi on 6 February 1975. Note the open wingtip speed brakes. (Masumi Wada via the Mick Roth Collection)

Two A-6As and a single A-6B (149957, in rear) drop 500-pound bombs over Vietnam. (U.S. Navy via Tony Thornborough)

An A-6A (151785) from VA-85 prepares to cat from the USS Kitty Hawk *on a strike against North Vietnam. (U.S. Navy via Tony Thornborough)*

ENGINE OPERATION DANGER AREAS

NOISE

EXHAUST BLAST

IDLE POWER — MAXIMUM POWER

ENGINE EXHAUST BLAST DANGER AREA (KEEP OUT)

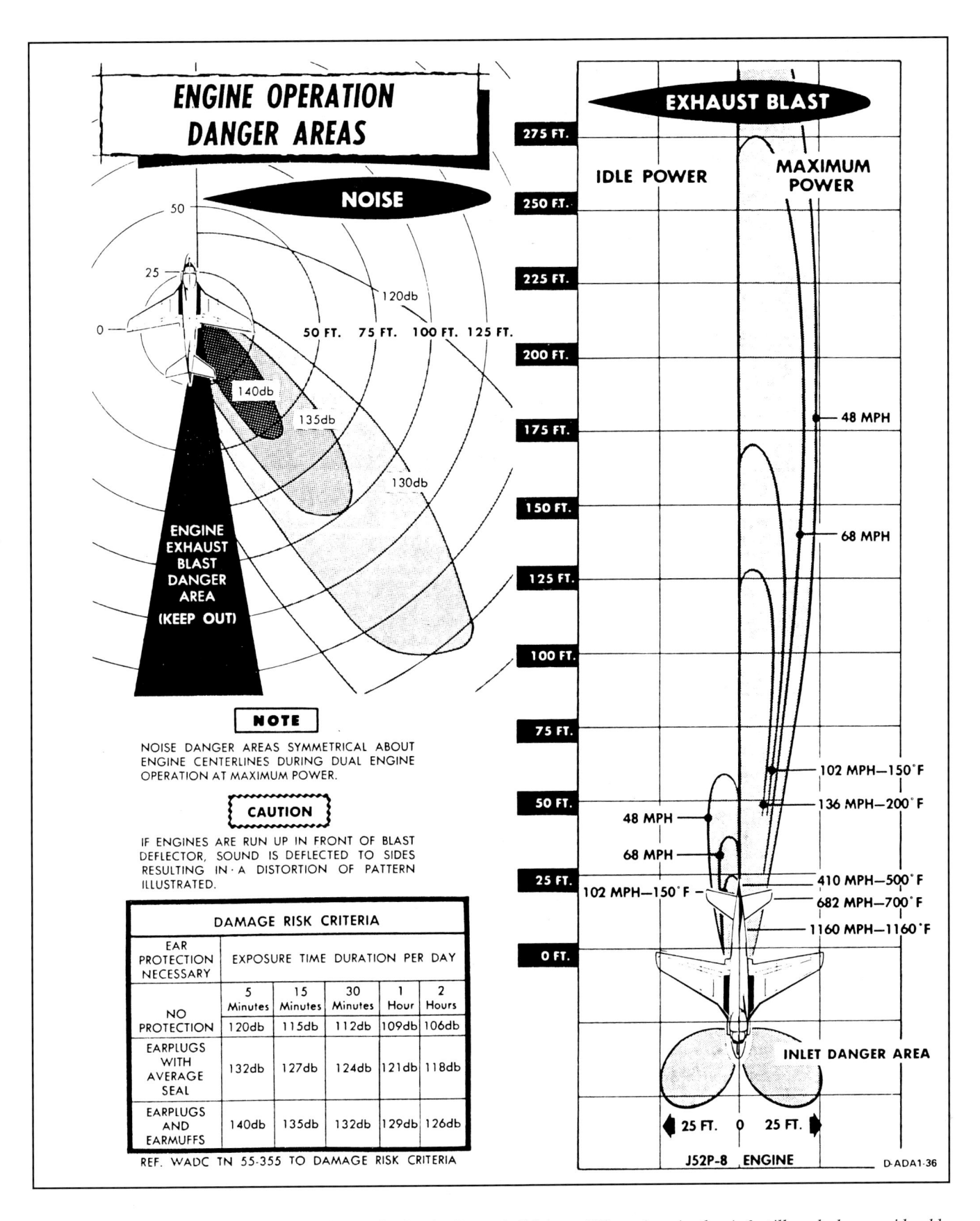

NOTE

NOISE DANGER AREAS SYMMETRICAL ABOUT ENGINE CENTERLINES DURING DUAL ENGINE OPERATION AT MAXIMUM POWER.

CAUTION

IF ENGINES ARE RUN UP IN FRONT OF BLAST DEFLECTOR, SOUND IS DEFLECTED TO SIDES RESULTING IN A DISTORTION OF PATTERN ILLUSTRATED.

DAMAGE RISK CRITERIA					
EAR PROTECTION NECESSARY	EXPOSURE TIME DURATION PER DAY				
	5 Minutes	15 Minutes	30 Minutes	1 Hour	2 Hours
NO PROTECTION	120db	115db	112db	109db	106db
EARPLUGS WITH AVERAGE SEAL	132db	127db	124db	121db	118db
EARPLUGS AND EARMUFFS	140db	135db	132db	129db	126db

REF. WADC TN 55-355 TO DAMAGE RISK CRITERIA

Exhaust blast distances: 48 MPH at 175 FT; 68 MPH at 150 FT; 102 MPH–150°F; 136 MPH–200°F; 48 MPH; 68 MPH; 102 MPH–150°F; 410 MPH–500°F; 682 MPH–700°F; 1160 MPH–1160°F

INLET DANGER AREA — 25 FT. 0 25 FT.

J52P-8 ENGINE

D-ADA1-36

Although comparatively small by today's standards, the Pratt & Whitney J52 engines in the A-6 still packed a considerable punch. This diagram shows the danger areas around the aircraft along with some figures describing the temperature and velocity of the exhaust gases. (U.S. Navy)

GRUMMAN A-6 INTRUDER

A pair of A-6As from VA-75 on the USS Saratoga during her Mediterranean cruise in December 1975. Note the empty multiple ejection racks (MERs) on the outboard pylons and the plastic covers over the air intakes. (Naval Historical Center)

An A-6A (155685) from VA-115 on 27 December 1974 approaching NAF Atsugi, Japan. (Masumi Wada via the Mick Roth Collection)

An A-6A (151812) from test squadron VX-5 shows a MER full of 500-pound bombs. Note the details of the wing fold mechanism. (Mick Roth Collection)

An A-6A (155688) sits in the storage yard at Davis-Monthan AFB during March 1977. The aircraft had last been assigned to VA-42. It is not unusual for aircraft to be stored temporarily while awaiting modification or reassignment to a new unit. (Mick Roth Collection)

Another VA-115 A-6A (155718) on 18 February 1975 at Atsugi with Mt. Fuji in the background. (Jack R. Bol via the Mick Roth Collection)

An early A-6A (149937) at China Lake on 19 May 1977. Note the open access ladder and speed brakes. (Roy Lock via the Mick Roth Collection)

GRUMMAN A-6 INTRUDER

27

A trio of A-6As from VA-35 from USS Enterprise *loaded with 500-pound bombs on a mission over Southeast Asia.* (U.S. Navy via Tony Thornborough)

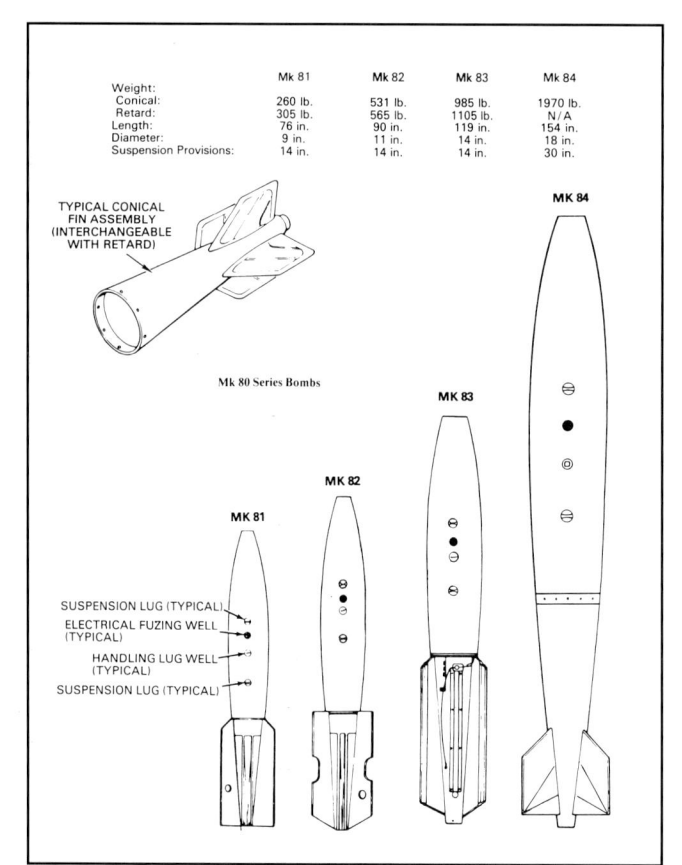

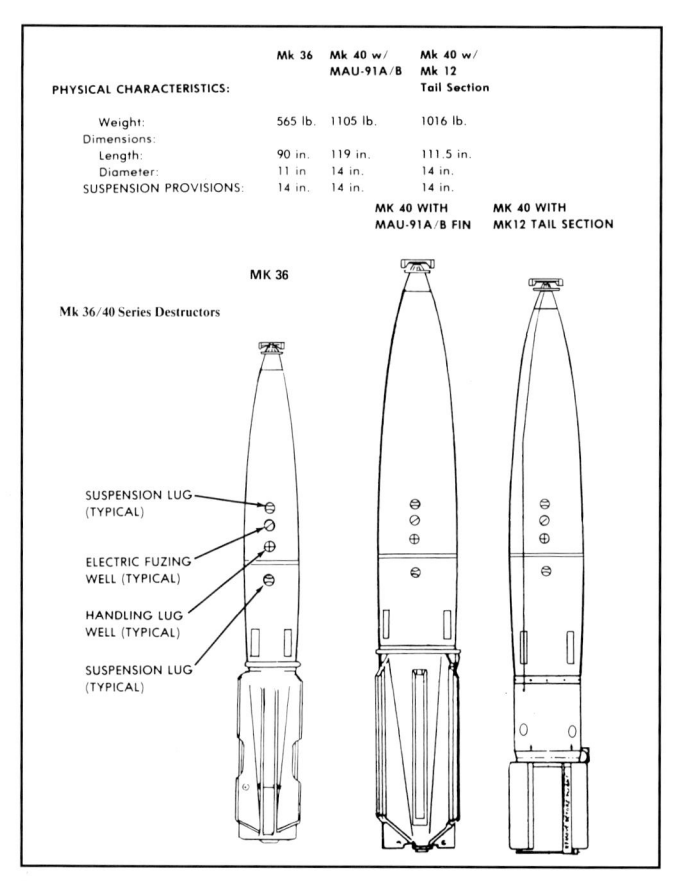

	Mk 81	Mk 82	Mk 83	Mk 84
Weight:				
Conical:	260 lb.	531 lb.	985 lb.	1970 lb.
Retard:	305 lb.	565 lb.	1105 lb.	N/A
Length:	76 in.	90 in.	119 in.	154 in.
Diameter:	9 in.	11 in.	14 in.	18 in.
Suspension Provisions:	14 in.	14 in.	14 in.	30 in.

Mk 80 Series Bombs

	Mk 36	Mk 40 w/ MAU-91A/B	Mk 40 w/ Mk 12 Tail Section
PHYSICAL CHARACTERISTICS:			
Weight:	565 lb.	1105 lb.	1016 lb.
Dimensions:			
Length:	90 in.	119 in.	111.5 in.
Diameter:	11 in.	14 in.	14 in.
SUSPENSION PROVISIONS:	14 in.	14 in.	14 in.

Mk 36/40 Series Destructors

The primary offensive armament of the A-6 for many years was the Mk 80 series of "iron bombs" and the Mk 36/40 series of "destructors." The destructors were meant for use as mines and were always delivered in a retarded mode. (U.S. Navy)

A staged publicity photo of six A-6As from VA-75 during the early 1970s. The black radomes would eventually give way to lighter colors. (U.S. Navy via Tony Thornborough)

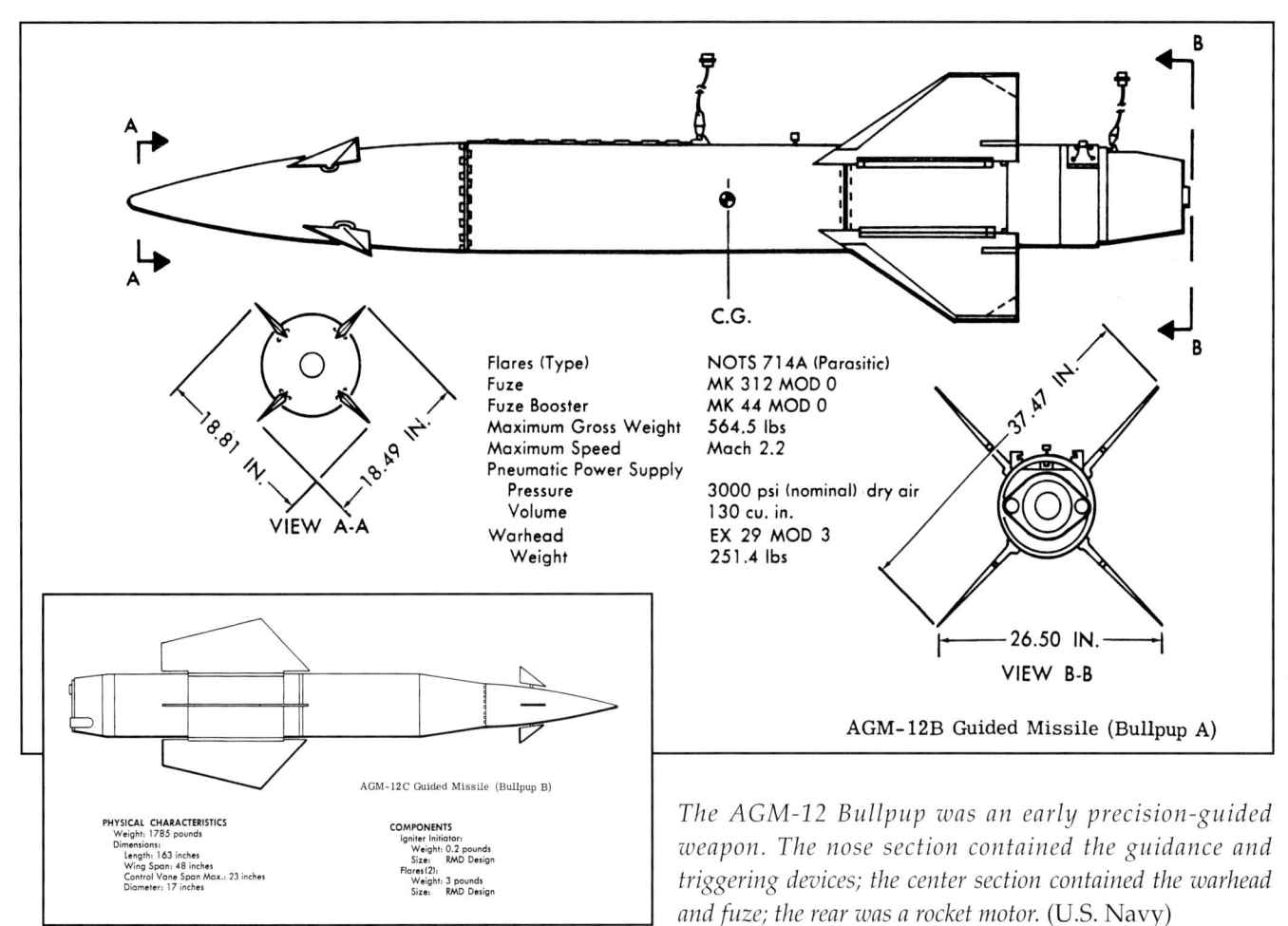

Flares (Type)	NOTS 714A (Parasitic)
Fuze	MK 312 MOD 0
Fuze Booster	MK 44 MOD 0
Maximum Gross Weight	564.5 lbs
Maximum Speed	Mach 2.2
Pneumatic Power Supply	
Pressure	3000 psi (nominal) dry air
Volume	130 cu. in.
Warhead	EX 29 MOD 3
Weight	251.4 lbs

AGM-12B Guided Missile (Bullpup A)

AGM-12C Guided Missile (Bullpup B)

PHYSICAL CHARACTERISTICS
Weight: 1785 pounds
Dimensions:
  Length: 163 inches
  Wing Span: 48 inches
  Control Vane Span Max.: 23 inches
  Diameter: 17 inches

COMPONENTS
Igniter Initiator:
  Weight: 0.2 pounds
  Size: RMD Design
Flares (2):
  Weight: 3 pounds
  Size: RMD Design

The AGM-12 Bullpup was an early precision-guided weapon. The nose section contained the guidance and triggering devices; the center section contained the warhead and fuze; the rear was a rocket motor. (U.S. Navy)

GRUMMAN A-6 INTRUDER

An A-6A from VA-75 about to trap after operations over Vietnam. Note the open wingtip speed brakes, the trailing edge flaps, and the deployed tail hook. (U.S. Navy via the Tony Thornborough Collection)

The Rockwell International XAGM-53A Condor was tested on an A-6A. The missile required a data link during the initial phases of flight — the data link pod was carried on the centerline station. (Rockwell International via the Tony Thornborough Collection)

A-6A ELECTRONIC EQUIPMENT ARRANGEMENT

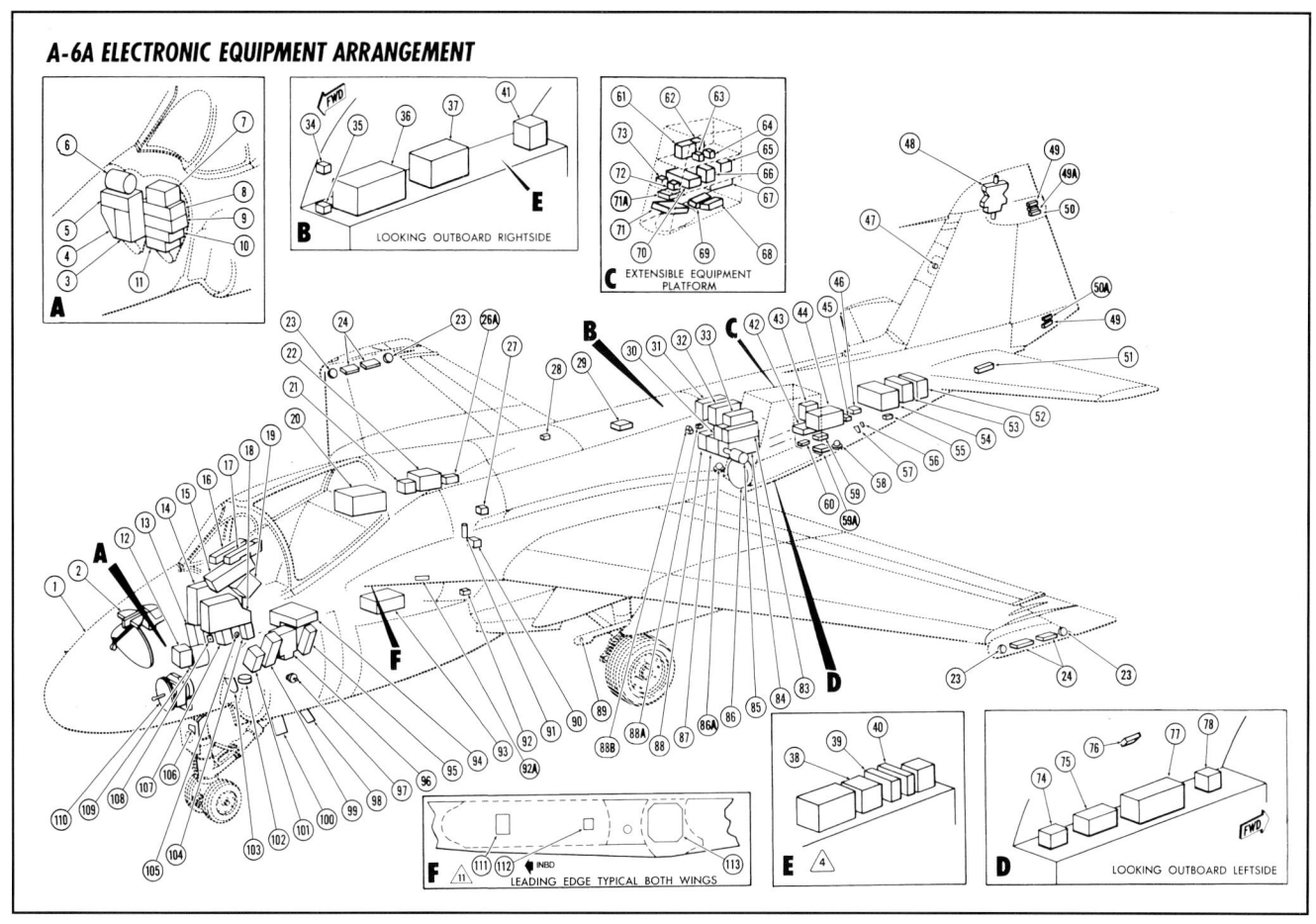

The A-6 was among the first Navy aircraft to carry a wide range of electronic equipment. In fact, the electronics were the entire rationale for the A-6 existing. Although most of the equipment that needed regular maintenance was located either in the bird cage or under the radome, other less-sensitive equipment was scattered throughout the aircraft — more so in later years as additional equipment was added that the designers had not anticipated. This drawing shows both the ALQ-100 and ALQ-126 ECM equipment, although only one or the other was carried by any individual aircraft. (U.S. Navy)

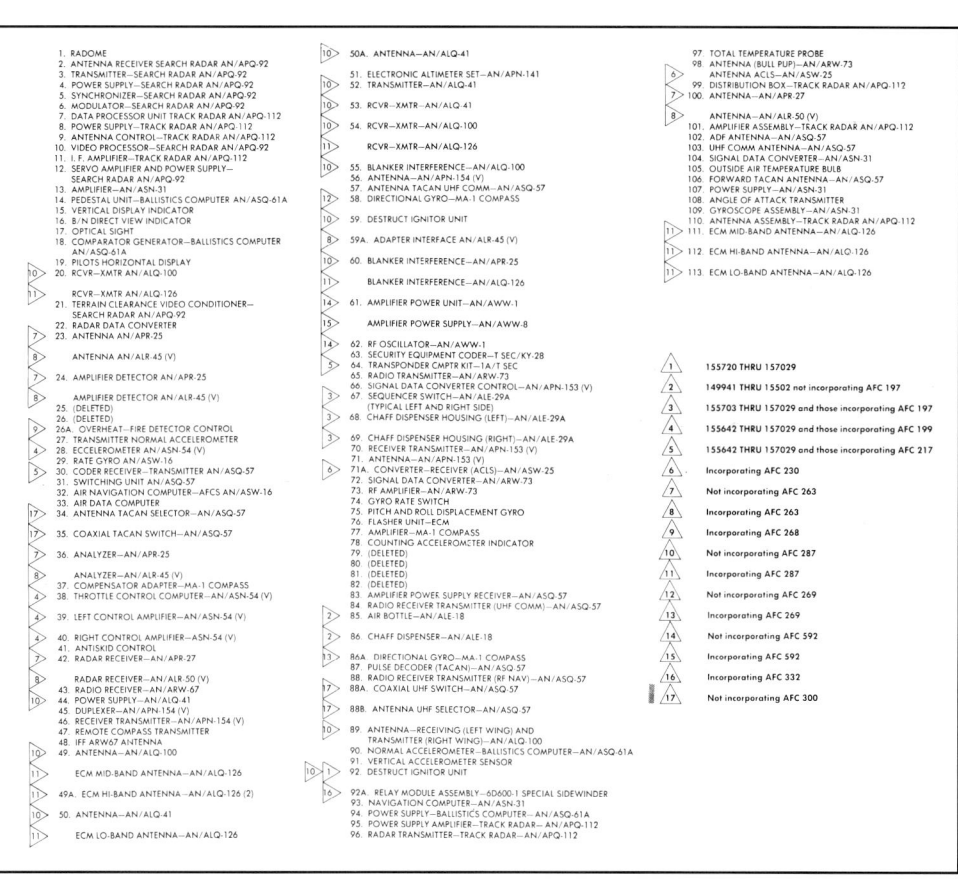

1. RADOME
2. ANTENNA RECEIVER SEARCH RADAR AN/APQ-92
3. TRANSMITTER—SEARCH RADAR AN/APQ-92
4. POWER SUPPLY—SEARCH RADAR AN/APQ-92
5. SYNCHRONIZER—SEARCH RADAR AN/APQ-92
6. MODULATOR—SEARCH RADAR AN/APQ-92
7. DATA PROCESSOR UNIT TRACK RADAR AN/APQ-112
8. POWER SUPPLY—TRACK RADAR AN/APQ-112
9. ANTENNA CONTROL—TRACK RADAR AN/APQ-112
10. VIDEO PROCESSOR—SEARCH RADAR AN/APQ-112
11. I. F. AMPLIFIER—TRACK RADAR AN/APQ-112
12. SERVO AMPLIFIER AND POWER SUPPLY—SEARCH RADAR AN/APQ-92
13. AMPLIFIER—AN/ASN-31
14. PEDESTAL UNIT—BALLISTICS COMPUTER AN/ASQ-61A
15. VERTICAL DISPLAY INDICATOR
16. OPTICAL SIGHT
17. COMPARATOR GENERATOR—BALLISTICS COMPUTER AN/ASQ-61A
18. B/N DIRECT VIEW INDICATOR
19. PILOTS HORIZONTAL DISPLAY
20. RCVR—XMTR AN/ALQ-100
   RCVR—XMTR AN/ALQ-126
21. TERRAIN CLEARANCE VIDEO CONDITIONER—SEARCH RADAR AN/APQ-92
22. RADAR DATA CONVERTER
23. ANTENNA AN/APR-25
   ANTENNA AN/ALR-45 (V)
24. AMPLIFIER DETECTOR AN/APR-25
   AMPLIFIER DETECTOR AN/ALR-45 (V)
25. (DELETED)
26. (DELETED)
26A. OVERHEAT—FIRE DETECTOR CONTROL
27. TRANSMITTER NORMAL ACCELEROMETER
28. ECCELEROMETER—AN/ASN-54 (V)
29. RATE GYRO AN/ASW-16
30. CODER RECEIVER—TRANSMITTER AN/ASQ-57
31. SWITCHING UNIT AN/ASQ-57
32. AIR NAVIGATION COMPUTER—AFCS AN/ASW-16
33. AIR DATA COMPUTER
34. COAXIAL TACAN SELECTOR—AN/ASQ-57
35. COAXIAL TACAN SWITCH—AN/ASQ-57
36. ANALYZER—AN/APR-25
37. ANALYZER—AN/ALR-45 (V)
   COMPENSATOR ADAPTER—MA-1 COMPASS
38. THROTTLE CONTROL COMPUTER—AN/ASN-54 (V)
39. LEFT CONTROL AMPLIFIER—AN/ASN-54 (V)
40. RIGHT CONTROL AMPLIFIER—AN/ASN-54 (V)
41. ANTISKID CONTROL
42. RADAR RECEIVER—AN/APR-27
43. RADIO RECEIVER—AN/ALR-50 (V)
44. RADIO RECEIVER—AN/ARW-67
45. POWER SUPPLY—AN/ALQ-41
46. DUPLEXER—AN/APN-154 (V)
47. RECEIVER TRANSMITTER—AN/APN-154 (V)
48. REMOTE COMPASS TRANSMITTER
49. IFF ARW67 ANTENNA
49A. ANTENNA—AN/ALQ-100
   ECM MID-BAND ANTENNA—AN/ALQ-126
49A. ECM HI-BAND ANTENNA—AN/ALQ-126 (2)
50. ANTENNA—AN/ALQ-41
   ECM LO-BAND ANTENNA—AN/ALQ-126

50A. ANTENNA—AN/ALQ-41
51. ELECTRONIC ALTIMETER SET—AN/APN-141
52. TRANSMITTER—AN/ALQ-41
53. RCVR—XMTR—AN/ALQ-41
54. RCVR—XMTR—AN/ALQ-100
   RCVR—XMTR—AN/ALQ-126
55. BLANKER INTERFERENCE—AN/ALQ-100
56. ANTENNA—AN/APN-154 (V)
57. ANTENNA TACAN UHF COUPLER—AN/ASQ-57
58. DIRECTIONAL GYRO—MA-1 COMPASS
59. DESTRUCT IGNITOR UNIT
59A. ADAPTER INTERFACE—AN/ALR-45 (V)
60. BLANKER INTERFERENCE—AN/APR-25
   BLANKER INTERFERENCE—AN/ALQ-126
61. AMPLIFIER POWER UNIT—AN/AWW-1
   AMPLIFIER POWER SUPPLY—AN/AWW-8
62. RF OSCILLATOR—AN/AWW-1
63. SECURITY EQUIPMENT CODER—AN/T SEC/KY-28
64. TRANSPONDER CMPTR KIT—1A/T SEC
65. RADIO TRANSMITTER—AN/ARW-73
66. SIGNAL DATA CONVERTER RADAR CONTROL—AN/APN-153 (V)
67. SEQUENCER SWITCH—AN/ALE-29A (TYPICAL LEFT AND RIGHT SIDE)
68. CHAFF DISPENSER HOUSING (LEFT)—AN/ALE-29A
69. CHAFF DISPENSER HOUSING (RIGHT)—AN/ALE-29A
70. RECEIVER TRANSMITTER—AN/APN-153 (V)
71. CONVERTER—RECEIVER AN/ASW-25
71A. SIGNAL DATA CONVERTER—AN/ARW-73
72. RF AMPLIFIER—AN/ARW-73
73. GYRO RATE SWITCH
74. PITCH AND ROLL DISPLACEMENT GYRO
75. FLASHER UNIT—ECM
76. AMPLIFIER—MA-1 COMPASS
77. COUNTING ACCELEROMETER INDICATOR
78. (DELETED)
79. (DELETED)
80. (DELETED)
81. (DELETED)
82. AMPLIFIER POWER SUPPLY RECEIVER—AN/ASQ-57
83. RADIO RECEIVER TRANSMITTER (UHF COMM)—AN/ASQ-57
84. AIR BOTTLE—AN/ALE-18
85. CHAFF DISPENSER—AN/ALE-18
86. DIRECTIONAL GYRO—MA-1 COMPASS
86A. PULSE DECODER (TACAN)
87. RADIO RECEIVER TRANSMITTER (RF NAV)—AN/ASQ-57
88. COAXIAL UHF SWITCH—AN/ASQ-57
88A. ANTENNA UHF SELECTOR—AN/ASQ-57
89. ANTENNA—RECEIVING (LEFT WING) AND TRANSMITTER (RIGHT WING)
90. NORMAL ACCELEROMETER—BALLISTICS COMPUTER—AN/ASQ-61A
91. VERTICAL ACCELEROMETER SENSOR
92. DESTRUCT IGNITOR UNIT
92A. RELAY MODULE ASSEMBLY—6D600-1 SPECIAL SIDEWINDER
93. NAVIGATION COMPUTER—AN/ASN-31
94. POWER SUPPLY—BALLISTICS COMPUTER—AN/ASQ-61A
95. POWER SUPPLY AMPLIFIER—TRACK RADAR—AN/APQ-112
96. RADAR TRANSMITTER—TRACK RADAR—AN/APQ-112

97. TOTAL TEMPERATURE PROBE
98. ANTENNA (BULL PUP)—AN/ARW-73
   ANTENNA ACLS—AN/ASW-25
99. DISTRIBUTION BOX—TRACK RADAR AN/APQ-112
100. ANTENNA—AN/ASN-31
   ANTENNA—AN/ALR-50 (V)
101. AMPLIFIER ASSEMBLY—TRACK RADAR AN/APQ-112
102. ADF ANTENNA
103. UHF COMM ANTENNA—AN/ASQ-57
104. SIGNAL DATA CONVERTER—AN/ASN-31
105. OUTSIDE AIR TEMPERATURE BULB
106. FORWARD TACAN ANTENNA—AN/ASN-31
107. POWER SUPPLY—AN/ASQ-57
108. ANGLE OF ATTACK TRANSMITTER
109. GYROSCOPE ASSEMBLY—AN/ASN-31
110. ANTENNA ASSEMBLY—TRACK RADAR AN/APQ-112
111. ECM MID-BAND ANTENNA—AN/ALQ-126
112. ECM HI-BAND ANTENNA—AN/ALQ-126
113. ECM LO-BAND ANTENNA—AN/ALQ-126

1. 155720 THRU 157029
2. 149941 THRU 155502 not incorporating AFC 197
3. 155703 THRU 157029 and those incorporating AFC 197
4. 155642 THRU 157029 and those incorporating AFC 199
5. 155642 THRU 157029 and those incorporating AFC 217
6. Incorporating AFC 230
7. Not incorporating AFC 263
8. Incorporating AFC 263
9. Incorporating AFC 268
10. Not incorporating AFC 287
11. Incorporating AFC 287
12. Incorporating AFC 269
13. Incorporating AFC 269
14. Not incorporating AFC 592
15. Incorporating AFC 592
16. Incorporating AFC 332
17. Not incorporating AFC 300

GRUMMAN A-6 INTRUDER

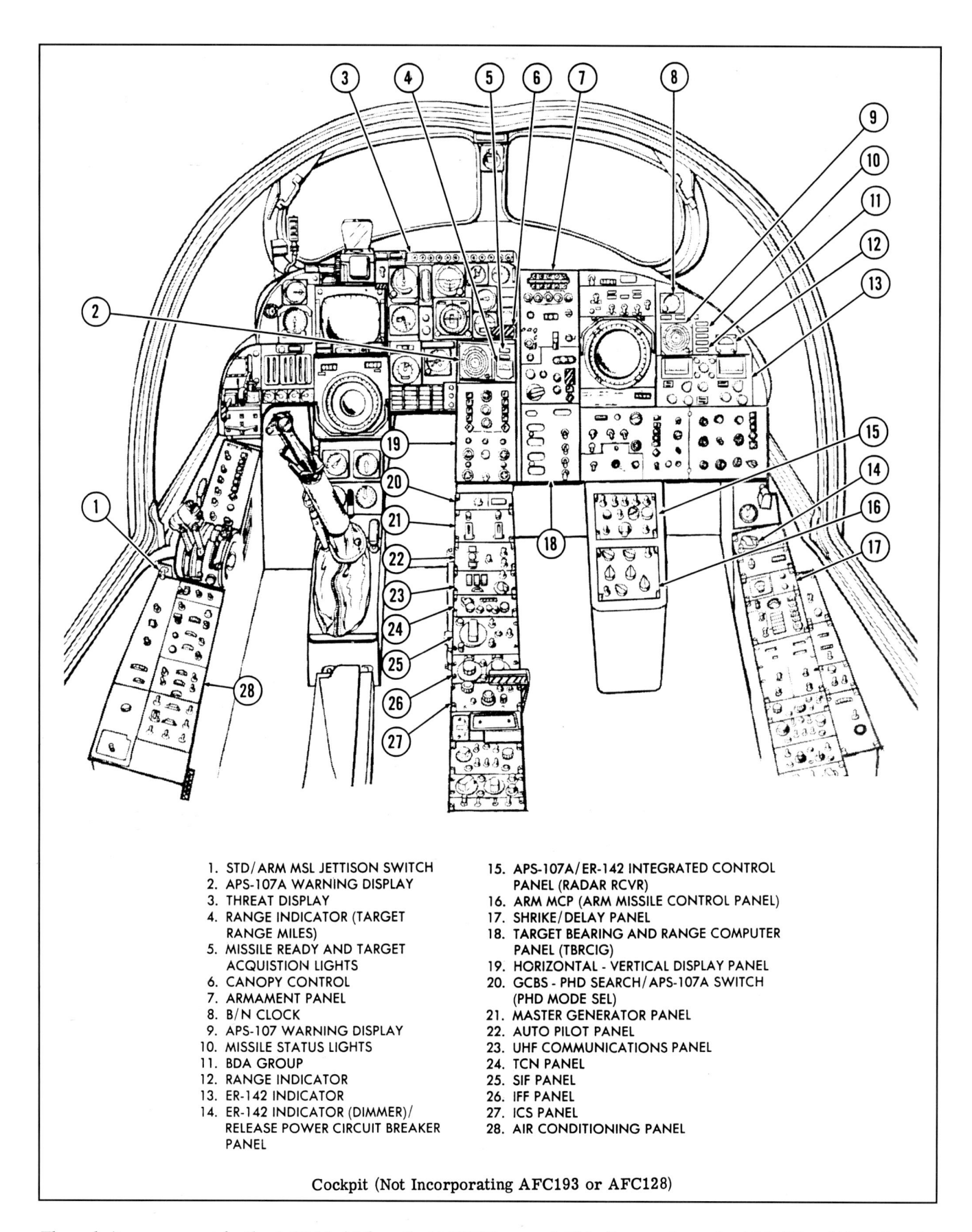

1. STD/ARM MSL JETTISON SWITCH
2. APS-107A WARNING DISPLAY
3. THREAT DISPLAY
4. RANGE INDICATOR (TARGET RANGE MILES)
5. MISSILE READY AND TARGET ACQUISITION LIGHTS
6. CANOPY CONTROL
7. ARMAMENT PANEL
8. B/N CLOCK
9. APS-107 WARNING DISPLAY
10. MISSILE STATUS LIGHTS
11. BDA GROUP
12. RANGE INDICATOR
13. ER-142 INDICATOR
14. ER-142 INDICATOR (DIMMER)/ RELEASE POWER CIRCUIT BREAKER PANEL
15. APS-107A/ER-142 INTEGRATED CONTROL PANEL (RADAR RCVR)
16. ARM MCP (ARM MISSILE CONTROL PANEL)
17. SHRIKE/DELAY PANEL
18. TARGET BEARING AND RANGE COMPUTER PANEL (TBRCIG)
19. HORIZONTAL - VERTICAL DISPLAY PANEL
20. GCBS - PHD SEARCH/APS-107A SWITCH (PHD MODE SEL)
21. MASTER GENERATOR PANEL
22. AUTO PILOT PANEL
23. UHF COMMUNICATIONS PANEL
24. TCN PANEL
25. SIF PANEL
26. IFF PANEL
27. ICS PANEL
28. AIR CONDITIONING PANEL

Cockpit (Not Incorporating AFC193 or AFC128)

The cockpit arrangement for the A-6B Mod 0 from the NATOPS manual. This diagram shows the APS-107 and ER-142 radar warning systems and both Shrike and Standard ARM control panels. (U.S. Navy)

SPECIALIZED 3 INTRUDERS

A FEW ODD-BALLS FILL IMPORTANT NICHES

Not surprisingly, the A-6 was tapped to fill a few niches other than the all-weather attack role it had been designed for. Perhaps the best known of these is outside the scope of this book. The EA-6A Electric Intruder was optimized for electronic warfare — specifically to jam enemy radar and communications. Eventually 13 A-6As (BuNos 147865, 148616, 148618, 149475, 149477/149478, 149935, and 151595/151600) would be modified into EA-6As (or EA-6A test aircraft) and 15 purpose-built EA-6As would also be manufactured. Three A-6As (BuNos 148615, 149479, and 149481) would also serve as test aircraft for the EA-6B program. Two A-6As (BuNos 147866 and 147867) would be used as general-purpose test aircraft for most of their careers and would be redesignated NA-6A, the "N" signifying that the modifications were nonoperational and permanent. Three other distinct configurations were also based on the A-6A and are discussed in this chapter.

JA-6A

A single JA-6A (BuNo 151568) was modified for research into a Circulation Control Wing (CCW). Proof-of-concept trials were carried out by Grumman in 1979 using a revised wing having an increased radius leading-edge slat, fixed at 25 percent, and an extensively modified trailing edge composed of aluminum, steel, and titanium. A bleed-air assembly ducted hot air from the J52 engines out through slots on top of the modified trailing edge. The hot air adhered to the trailing edge, generating improved overall air circulation around the wing, and thus providing extra lift.

During 16 flights with the CCW, or Goanda-effect wing as it was also known, the JA-6 demonstrated it could land at 36,000 pounds using 1,000 feet less runway than normal, take off at a gross weight of 46,000 pounds with a ground roll 400 feet less than the typical 1,800-foot roll, and touch down at a mere 78 knots at 32,000 pounds. The external plumbing limited the A-6's top speed to around 250 knots and was not considered a serious production possibility. Nevertheless, it provided valuable research which might find possible future application on a dedicated STOL aircraft.

A-6B

Shrike-equipped A-4s flying IRON HAND missions demonstrated the potential to seek out and destroy enemy air defense radars. To further exploit this concept, 19 A-6As were modified into three different A-6B configurations specifically to destroy ground-based antiaircraft defenses.

The operational limitations of the AGM-45 Shrike convinced the Navy to look for a better solution. Development of the AGM-78 Standard ARM began during early 1966 in an effort to field, as quickly as possible, an antiradiation missile with longer range (i.e., capable of being fired at an SA-2 site from outside the GUIDELINE's operational envelope), a larger warhead, and a better

A single A-6A (151568) was modified to test a Circulation Control Wing (CCW) concept during 1979. Note the external plumbing under the fuselage — this severely limited the top speed of the modified aircraft, but did not seriously impact the test objectives. (Grumman via Tony Thornborough)

One of the early production A-6As (149481) was modified as an aerodynamic prototype of the new four-seat EA-6B. This aircraft incorporated all of the exterior modifications scheduled for the new variant, including the extended forward fuselage and modified vertical stabilizer, but did not include any of the electronics. Two other A-6As (148615 and 149479) were also modified into EA-6Bs and included all of the new ECM systems. The electronic warfare variants are sufficiently different that they will not be covered in this book — instead, a future volume of the WarbirdTECH Series *will be dedicated to the EA-6A and EA-6B. (Grumman via Tony Thornborough)*

Several A-6As were also modified into EA-6As — this aircraft (148618) was the prototype EA-6A. Note the large pods under the outer wing panels. These were not featured on production aircraft. The EA-6A modification was much less radical than the later EA-6B variant and retained a two-seat cockpit, although the forward fuselage has been extended to accommodate additional electronics. (Grumman via Tony Thornborough)

seeker than the Shrike. A survey of existing missiles quickly narrowed the choice to the General Dynamics (GD) Standard missile. Designed for fleet air defense as the Tartar and Terrier, the Standard possessed twice the range of Shrike yet was still small enough that a pair could be carried by an A-6-size aircraft.

The first AGM-78 air test vehicles were captive-carried on an A-6A on July 1966, followed by unpowered separation tests in August, and the first launch tests (with dummy guidance and control sections) in September. By the end of September 1966 the results of these tests were positive enough that a contract was issued to GD to integrate the Texas Instruments Shrike seeker with the Standard missile airframe. A more sophisticated seeker would be developed later.

When the A-6A was modified to carry the AGM-78A (Mod 0) missile, the APQ-112 track radar and ASQ-61A ballistics computer were removed. This left only the APQ-92 search radar and ASA-31 INS portions of the DIANE system, significantly limiting the A-6's normal attack capabilities.

Originally the Mod 0 aircraft used a Bendix APS-107A (rather than the APR-25) radar warning receiver, a Magnavox APR-27 launch warning receiver, and an ATI ER-142 panoramic receiver. The APS-107A was later upgraded to the APS-107B, and finally the APS-107 and ER-142 were replaced by the ALR-55 and ALR-57 which were NAFI upgrades of the APS-107 (essentially equivalent to the Air Force's APS-107E) and ER-142 (X-band coverage was incorporated in addition to S- and C-bands) respectively. Other new equipment included a target range

Modified A-6A Bureau Numbers

BuNo		Qty	Notes
JA-6A / NA-6A			
147866		1	(NA-6A)
147867		1	(NA-6A) A-6C Tests
151568		1	(JA-6A) CCW Modification
EA-6A			
147865		1	EA-6A Electronic Test Aircraft
148616		1	Converted to EA-6A
148618		1	Prototype EA-6A
149475		1	Converted to EA-6A
149477	– 149478	2	Converted to EA-6A
149935		1	NEA-6A Test Aircraft
151595	– 151600	6	Converted to EA-6A
EA-6B			
148615		1	EA-6B Electronic Test Aircraft
149479		1	EA-6B Full-up Development Aircraft
149481		1	EA-6B Aerodynamic Demonstrator
A-6B			
149944		1	Mod 1 Standard ARM
149949		1	Mod 0 Standard ARM
149955		1	Mod 1 Standard ARM
149957		1	Mod 0 Standard ARM
151558	– 151565	8	Mod 0 Standard ARM
151591		1	Mod 1 Standard ARM
151820		1	Mod 1 Standard ARM
152616	– 152617	2	Mod 1 Standard ARM
155628	– 155630	3	PAT/ARM
A-6C			
155647	– 155648	2	
155653		1	
155660		1	
155662		1	
155667		1	
155670		1	
155674		1	
155676		1	
155681		1	
155684		1	
155688		1	

A-6B MOD 1

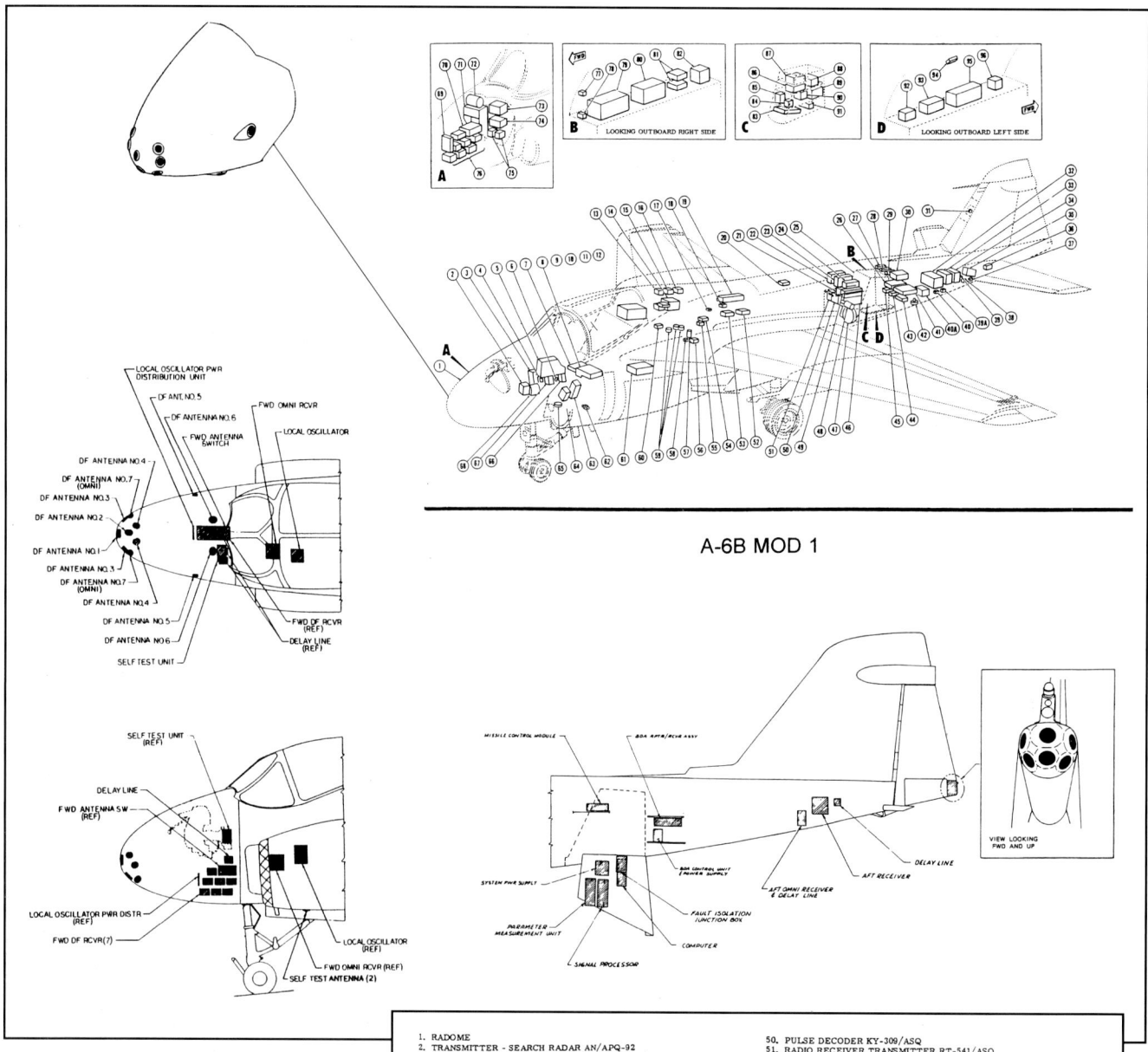

The A-6B Mod 1 aircraft carried an array of direction finding antennas on the nose and tail as shown here. The normal APQ-112 track radar was removed to make room for the DF receivers, and most of the DIANE equipment was removed from the bird cage to make room for other equipment. Only the APQ-92 search radar and ASA-31 inertial navigation system were left intact, severely limiting the A-6B's conventional strike capabilities. It did not really matter, however, since the aircraft were intended solely to fire the Standard ARM against SAM and AAA radars. (U.S. Navy)

1. RADOME
2. TRANSMITTER - SEARCH RADAR AN/APQ-92
3. ELECTRONIC CONTROL AMPLIFIER AM-2750/ASN-31
4. SIGNAL DATA CONVERTER CV-1014/ASN-31
5. COMPARATOR GENERATOR - BALLISTICS COMPUTER AN/ASQ-61
6. OUTSIDE AIR TEMPERATURE BULB
7. DISPLAY JUNCTION BOX
8. POWER SUPPLY - BALLISTICS COMPUTER AN/ASQ-61A
9. DIM AND TEST BOX
10. ECM RECEIVER TRANSMITTER AN/ALQ-100
11. TERRAIN CLEARANCE VIDEO CONDITIONER MX-4948/AVA-1
12. RIGHT JUNCTION BOX FOR GENERATOR
13. WEAPON RELAY MODULE STATION 3
14. RADAR DATA CONVERTER CV-1607/AVA-1
15. WEAPON RELAY MODULE STATION 2 AND 4
16. WEAPON RELAY MODULE STATION 1 AND 5
17. NULL DETECTOR
18. ENCODER JUNCTION BOX
19. AC DC RELAY BOX
20. RATE GYRO AFCS AN/ASW-16
21. CODER RECEIVER TRANSMITTER KY-308/ASQ OR KY-533/ASQ
22. SWITCHING UNIT SA-629/ARC
23. AIR NAVIGATION COMPUTER CP-567/ASW-16
24. AIR DATA COMPUTER
25. AN/APR-27
26. RADAR RECEIVER R-1412/APR-27
27. SIGNAL DATA CONVERTER CV-890/ARW-73
28. RADIO FREQUENCY AMPLIFIER AM-2368/ARW-73
29. RADIO TRANSMITTER T-714/ARW-73
30. POWER SUPPLY PP-3067/ALQ-41
31. REMOTE COMPASS TRANSMITTER
32. ECM RECEIVER TRANSMITTER AN/ALQ-100
33. TRANSMITTER AN/ALQ-41
34. RECEIVER TRANSMITTER AN/ALQ-41
35. DF RECEIVER R-1611/APS-118
36. DELAY LINE AN/APS-118
37. ELECTRONIC ALTIMETER SET APN-141(V)
38. OMNI RECEIVER R-1612/APS-118
39. DELAY LINE AN/APS-118
39A. BLANKER PULSE AMPLIFIER AN/ALQ-41
40. INTERFERENCE BLANKER AN/ALQ-100
40A. DELAY LINE
41. BDA REPEATER-RECEIVER
42. DIRECTIONAL GYRO - MA-1 COMPASS
43. KY-28
44. BDA CONTROL UNIT
45. BDA POWER SUPPLY
46. RADIO RECEIVER TRANSMITTER RT-542/ASQ
47. CHAFF DISPENSER - AN/ALE-18
48. AIR BOTTLE - AN/ALE-18
49. AMPLIFIER - MA-1 COMPASS
50. PULSE DECODER KY-309/ASQ
51. RADIO RECEIVER TRANSMITTER RT-541/ASQ
52. STANDARD ARM MISSILE MODULE
53. SHRIKE RELAY BOX
54. LEFT JUNCTION BOX FOR GENERATOR
55. TRANSMITTER NORMAL ACCELEROMETER - AFCS AN/ASW-16
56. LEFT SUPERVISORY REGULATOR CONTROL PANEL FOR GENERATOR
57. VERTICAL ACCELEROMETER SENSOR
58. NORMAL ACCELEROMETER - BALLISTICS COMPUTER AN/ASQ-61A
59. LINE CONTACTORS FOR GENERATOR CONTROL PANEL
60. RIGHT SUPERVISORY REGULATOR CONTROL PANEL FOR GENERATOR
61. NAVIGATION COMPUTER CP-751/ASN-31
62. AMPLIFIER - MA-1 COMPASS
63. LOCAL OSCILLATOR O-1541/APS-118
64. FORWARD OMNI RECEIVER R-1612/APS-118
65. ADF ANTENNA - AN/ASQ-57
66. SIGNAL DATA CONVERTER - AN/ASN-31
67. POWER SUPPLY - AN/ASN-31
68. GYROSCOPE ASSEMBLY - AN/ASN-31
69. LO POWER DISTRIBUTION UNIT MX-8338/APS-118
70. POWER SUPPLY PP-2881/APS-118
71. ELECTRICAL SYNCHRONIZER SN-297/APQ-92
72. RADAR MODULATOR MD-402/APQ92
73. DATA PROCESSOR UNIT CP/APQ-88
74. SELF TEST UNIT ON-74/APS-118
75. DELAY LINES AN/APS-118
76. FORWARD D.F. RECEIVERS R-1610/APS-118 (7 REQ.)
77. DIPLEXER FILTER F-339/A
78. COAXIAL SWITCH SA-521/A
79. MISSILE CONTROL MODULE
80. COMPENSATOR-ADAPTER - MA-1 COMPASS
81. CONTROL PANEL - AN/ALR-15
82. ANTI SKID CONTROL
83. ANTENNA - AN/APN-153(V)
84. TIAS ISOLATION RELAY BOX
85. AMPLIFIER POWER SUPPLY AM-2014/AWW-1 AND RF OSCILLATOR O-562/AWW-1
86. SIGNAL PROCESSOR UNIT MX-8331/APS-118
87. PARAMETER MEASUREMENT UNIT MX-8335/APS-118
88. POWER SUPPLY PP-6261/APS-118
89. FAULT ISOLATION JUNCTION BOX AN/APS-118
90. COMPUTER CP-976/APS-118
91. DOPPLER SIGNAL DATA CONVERTER C-6182/APN-153(V)
92. GYRO RATE SWITCH
93. PITCH AND ROLL DISPLACEMENT GYRO
94. RECEIVER TRANSMITTER RT-680A/APN-153(V)
95. AMPLIFIER - MA-1 COMPASS
96. COUNTING ACCELEROMETER INDICATOR

and bearing computer, a bomb damage assessment unit, and a missile control assembly.

The first launch of an AGM-78 with a guidance section was in November 1966, but there's no indication that the aircraft was equipped with anything more than a "fire control panel" in the cockpit. The first launch from an A-6 equipped with an APS-107A was in March 1967, followed by a launch in July using both the APS-107 and ER-142.

Ten A-6As (BuNos 149949, 149957, and 151558–151565) were modified by Grumman Calverton, and the first reconfigured example (BuNo 149957) was redelivered to the Navy on 22 August 1967. Four aircraft were lost during operations, and the six survivors were later upgraded to A-6Es. The modified aircraft shared so little in common with the basic A-6A that in October 1967 they were redesignated A-6Bs by NAVAIR order 13100, using the designation of another proposed Air Force variant that was never built. These first 10 aircraft were, somewhat after the fact, known as A-6B Mod 0s, taking the name of the missile they were armed with.

Improvements to the A-6B continued with the introduction of the AGM-78B/Mod 1 missile in 1968. This version was fitted with a new Maxson broadband seeker, able to detect the growing range of SA-2 radar-operating frequencies as well as the latest Soviet-supplied ground control intercept and AAA radar. To make the most of the AGM-78B/Mod 1, the original (Mod 0) A-6Bs were quickly upgraded to "Mod 0 update" status by AFC 193. Grumman referred to these A-6Bs as Mod 0/1s since they could launch both Mod 0 and Mod 1 Standard ARMs.

The AGM-78/Mod 1 had several different launch modes depending on circumstances, making it significantly more flexible than Shrike. It could be programmed to turn to a certain bearing after launch and then seek to acquire the target. The B/N had absolutely no control of the ARM after launch, but if it had been locked on to a radar which subsequently shut down, it would continue to guide to the last known location of the radar. This might not ensure a hit, but it was an improvement over the Shrike which would have simply flown an unguided ballistic trajectory.

The Mod 0/1s were distributed throughout the fleet with two or three A-6Bs going to regular A-6A

A TIAS A-6B Mod 1 (151591) from VA-34 at NAS Oceana in June 1974. A careful examination of the nose will reveal the small DF antennas scattered around the radome, while similar antennas are visible on the extreme aft fuselage under the rudder. (Jerry Greer via the Robert F. Dorr Collection)

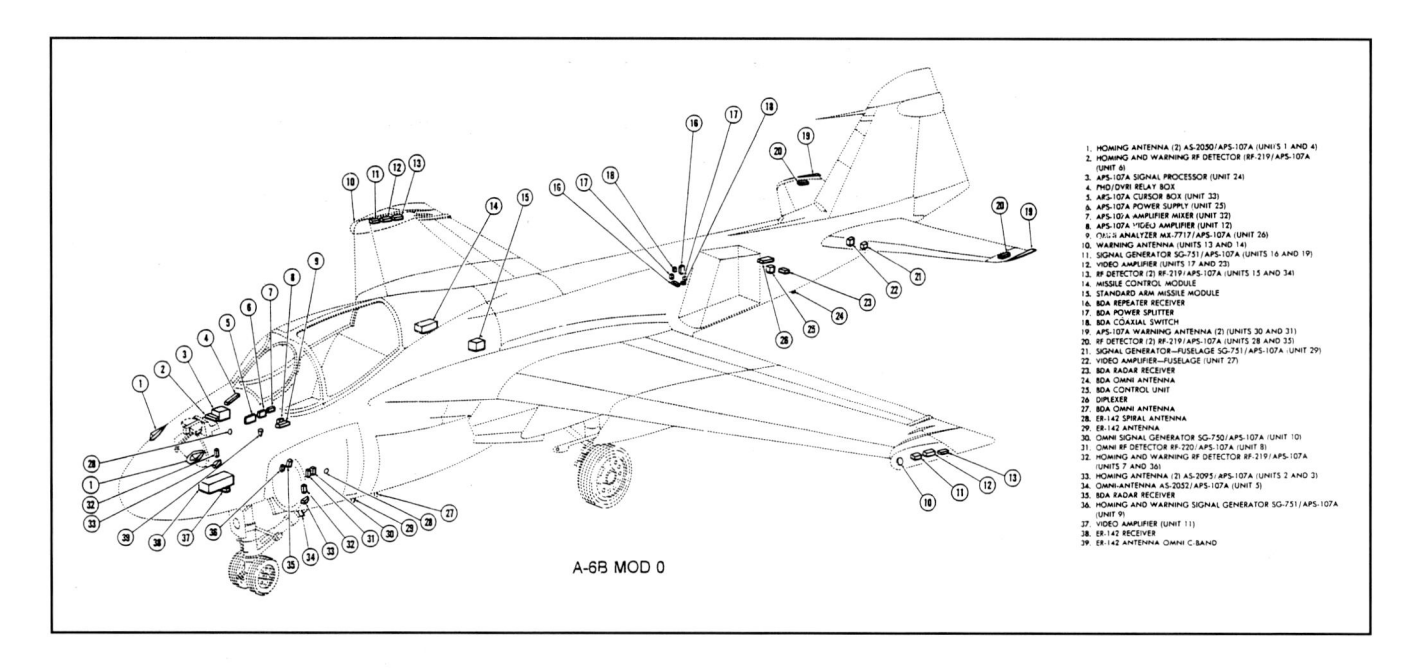

The location of the various specialized electronics in the A-6B Mod 0 (above) and Mod 0/1 (below). (U.S. Navy)

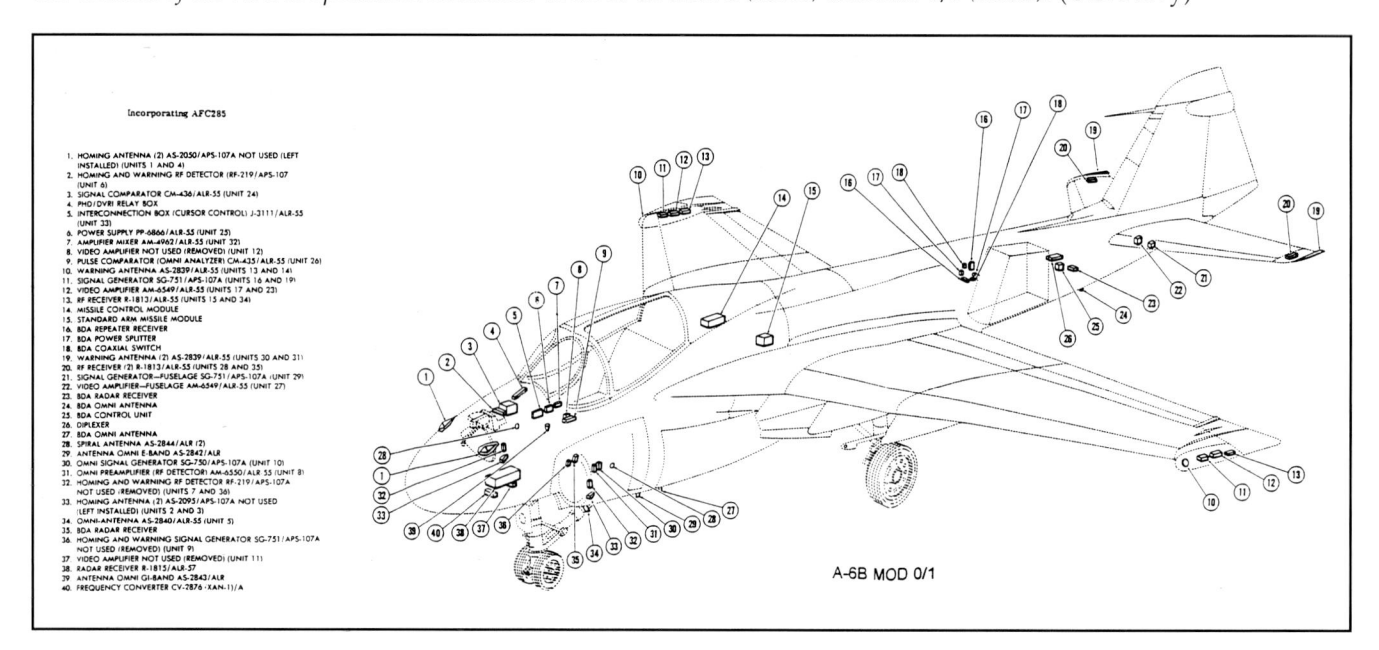

units. They saw combat service with at least five attack squadrons, including VA-52, VA-75, VA-85, VA-145, and VA-196. This wide distribution, often on a short-term loan basis, ensured that there were always at least three A-6Bs to support IRON HAND operations in Southeast Asia. The first operational use of the Mod 0 A-6B was by VA-75 flying from the USS *Kitty Hawk*, launching a AGM-78 against a live target in March 1968.

On 20 August 1968 VA-196 pilot LT Daniel C. Brandenstein was flying with the squadron flight surgeon, LT Bill Neal, Jr., when their A-6B (BuNo 151560) went in the water immediately after launch due to a flight control problem. Fortunately, both survived. VA-85 lost an A-6B (BuNo 151561) on 28 August 1968 on a night mission 10 miles southwest of Vinh, apparently after being hit by an SA-2. LTJG Robert Duncan and LTJG Allen Ashall were both listed as KIA (killed in action). Although these were the only two A-6Bs lost to date, a training syllabus was finally established at VA-42 in mid-1969, and a detachment from VA-165 were the first graduates on 12 November 1969.

Confidence rose as operational experience was gained and the A-6B Mod 0/1s soon found themselves committed to combat with increasing frequency, and with less restrictions on the employment of the Standard

ARM. The Mod 0s and 0/1s eventually accounted for several dozen SAM sites destroyed or damaged. Two other A-6Bs were lost, in October 1971 and July 1972, although neither occurred in Southeast Asia.

During February 1967, Johns Hopkins University's Applied Physics Laboratory (JHU-APL) had begun a feasibility study on the use of a passive receiver in conjunction with the APQ-112 radar. The goal was to add a radiating target detection and location capability to the A-6 without sacrificing or degrading any of the aircraft's existing navigation or weapons delivery capabilities.

Since SAM sites could not be easily located by the A-6's radar system, and passive ECM receivers could provide angular data but not range, JHU-APL's approach was to combine the two. An S-band homing receiver was integrated into the APQ-112's angle tracking circuitry and four blade-type antennas were mounted on the APQ-112 dish. Using phase interferometry techniques, the passive angle tracking (PAT) system determined the azimuth and elevation from the aircraft to an emitting FAN SONG radar and centered the radar antenna on the target. The APQ-112 then determined the slant range to the point defined by PAT. Data from the PAT and APQ-112 were supplied to the ASQ-61A ballistics computer in order to compute a firing solution.

The PAT system only operated in a narrow slice of S-band and had a very narrow look angle ahead of the aircraft. The A-6 also had an APR-25 radar homing and warning set for 360-degree warning, for coverage of threats outside of PAT's frequency range, and to resolve angular ambiguities inherent in phase interferometry. An angle gate circuit card was added to the APR-25 signal analyzer to define the boundaries of PAT's angular coverage for APR-25/PAT correlation purposes and to provide a target designation cursor on the APR-25 azimuth indicator. When a target was designated by the B/N, the data was sent to the Standard ARM missile control module (the interface between the AGM-78 and the aircraft avionics) and then to the missile itself. In addition to the PAT panels, a missile control panel (two panels when the aircraft were upgraded to use Mod 1 missiles) allowed the B/N to select various missile modes and, for Mod 1 missiles only, specify target frequency and PRF windows.

In November 1967 the first developmental version of PAT was installed in an A-6A (BuNo 152914) for testing. This A-6 was probably a VX-5 or NATC aircraft that was used only for testing and later demodified; it did

The A-6B PAT/ARM aircraft did not have the DF antennas around the radome. Instead, four small blade antennas were mounted on the dish of the APQ-112 antenna under the radome — these were not visible unless the radome was open. The AGM-78 Standard ARM shown here is a dummy round. (Robert F. Dorr Collection)

The cockpit of an A-6B Mod 0 (149957). (Grumman via Tony Thornborough)

not become one of the operational aircraft. The initial test phase revealed a number of problems that required JHU-APL to redesign portions of the system, but it showed enough promise for the Navy to authorize the modification of three A-6As (BuNos 155628–155630) to the PAT/ARM configuration on 30 June 1968. The initial A-6B PAT/ARM (BuNo 155628) first flew on 26 August 1968 with Al Quinby and A. J. Beck on board. All three aircraft were delivered to the fleet between April and June 1969 and spent their entire PAT careers in the Pacific, seeing action in SEA with VA-165 and VA-52, then later with VA-95 and VA-115.

Two of the three PAT/ARM A-6Bs (155629 and 155630) were delivered to NATC in April and May 1969 for Navy technical evaluation, which ran until the middle of July. The third was used for operational testing by VX-5. The improved PAT systems still had some problems that required more modifications by JHU-APL and Grumman, and at some point the aircraft were updated to carry the AGM-78B/Mod 1 missile. The PAT/ARM aircraft were taken into combat by VA-85 on a 1969–1970 cruise aboard the USS *Constellation* (CV-64) which included 12 new A-6As and two A-6B PAT aircraft. According to the *General Dynamics Standard ARM Summary of Tactical Operations Report*, the first PAT/ARM combat use was not until April 1970, by which time the Mod 1 capability had been incorporated.

The PAT/ARM aircraft originally had a modified APR-25 and an APR-27. Since the PAT airplanes were around for some time after Vietnam, they may have received the AFC-263 ALR-45/50 suite, but documentation to confirm this change has not been located. However, since the analog APR-25s in the PAT aircraft were not stock systems, it is possible that the additional angle gate circuit card was not compatible with the partially digital ALR-45.

The major task undertaken by the PAT/ARMs, in common with the Mod 0/1s, was to fly in support of BLUE TREE and ARREC missions. They echoed the Mod 0/1s' successes in continually forcing the enemy to shut down tracking radars, thereby enabling the U.S. aircraft to pass by unmolested. It was widely reported that no aircraft supported by an A-6B was attacked by enemy SAMs or radar directed AAA during its mission. When not passively intimidating the enemy, the aircraft were sent out on radarscope photography sorties to collect possible offset aim points for use in radar attacks by the use of a KD-2 camera tied to the DVRI.

The A-6Bs seldom launched their AGM-78s and frequently returned to the carrier with a full complement of missiles, something that presented a new problem. The 1,350 pound AGM-78 — too expensive to jettison — invariably pushed the A-6Bs over their maximum landing weight. This meant crews had to dump large quantities of fuel prior to landing on the carrier. Following a few close calls during the second PAT combat cruise, with engines on the point of flaming out as the A-6Bs took a wire, VA-165 declared the problem "a critical maximum trap fuel limitation" and requested a strengthened rear truss and tailhook that would allow landings up to 36,000 pounds. The go-ahead came in July 1970 when AFC 244 added the EA-6A tailhook assembly, effectively doubling the maximum trap fuel to 5,000 pounds. No further problems were encountered and the modification was incorporated into all the A-6Bs.

By far the more capable of the three A-6B variants were the aircraft equipped with the IBM APS-118 target identification & acquisition system (TIAS), generally known as Mod 1 aircraft. Six A-6As (BuNos 149944, 149955, 151591, 151820, 152616, and 152617) were modified by Grumman and reaccepted by the Navy between 30 April and 1 August 1970. The four surviving airframes were later upgraded to A-6Es.

The TIAS A-6Bs introduced much more sophisticated equipment into the IRON HAND mission via enhanced prelaunch missile programming, giving the crew a significant degree of control over the AGM-78B/Mod 1 for improved target acquisition in a high threat environment. This was made possible by the expanded integration of onboard systems — the APS-118, DIANE, and Standard ARM were interfaced with each other allowing the crew to make better use of the AGM-78's 35 mile stand-off attack potential. Externally, the TIAS A-6Bs were distinguished by the presence of a large array of radar-receiving antennas scattered all over the nose radome.

It appears that the Mod 1 aircraft were only assigned to VA-34 and VA-35. The single loss (BuNo 152616) was by VA-34 during peacetime operations in the Mediterranean. The remainder of the Mod 1s' time was spent in operational testing at Point Mugu or with General Dynamics at Lindbergh Field in San Diego, both in California.

The Mod 1 aircraft originally had the ALR-15 radar warning receiver and APR-27 launch warning receiver. The ALR-15 was more or less equivalent to the Air Force's nearly useless pre-Vietnam APS-54; it simply lit a left or right side warning light in the cockpit if it received any S-, C-, or X-band signals from one side of the aircraft or the other. The ALR-15 was replaced by the ALR-45 (a partially digital upgrade of the APR-25 RHAW set) and the APR-27 was replaced by the Magnavox ALR-50 in 1973 (AFC 263 Part 2). The APR-27 was essentially a one-dimensional system (SA-2 guidance only); the ALR-50 was an APR-27 upgrade with wider frequency coverage and logic which recognized the guidance signals of more types of SAMs.

A-6C

Another Intruder variant born out of the war in Southeast Asia was created in response to a very different need. While in pursuit of enemy traffic along the Ho Chi Minh Trail, DIANE exhibited a severe limitation — its search radar was simply unable to locate the enemy. The radar was designed to search and track in areas with radar-significant returns, such as ships, bridges, or other prominent landmarks. Trucks and bicycles in a jungle wilderness

The fourth A-6A (147867) was modified into an NA-6A TRIM development aircraft with the new sensors housed in two large angular pods under the out wing panels. Interestingly, this is the same locations that the original EA-6A development aircraft carried their new electronic equipment — in very similar pods. (Grumman via the Robert F. Dorr Collection)

twisted by sheer, tertiary stage limestone outcrops did not match this criterion. Visual attack was usually out of the question due to bad weather or the thick jungle canopy.

In an effort to solve this problem, the Navy initiated the development of the Trails and Roads Interdiction Multisensor (TRIM) system in 1967. TRIM finally emerged as an integrated electro-optic sensor package designed to complement the normal A-6 radars, taking advantage of recent advances in low-light level television (LLLTV) technology and forward-looking infrared (FLIR) sensors to extend the vision of strike crews into the dark and limited bad weather (clouds, but not necessarily rain).

Following an early combat evaluation of TRIM aboard four specially modified Lockheed AP-2H (redesignated OP-2E) Neptunes based at Cam Ranh Bay between September 1968 and June 1969, a single NA-6A (BuNo 147867) was equipped for trials. This aircraft carried its new sensors in bulky angular-shaped pods on the outboard wing pylons. When the TRIM sensors finally matured, they were integrated into a single detachable ventral fuselage cupola with aft-facing fins for improved directional stability. The same stronger tailhook assembly that had been fitted to the A-6B and EA-6A was included to accommodate the higher trap weight.

The new RCA LLLTV and Texas Instruments FLIR sensors were mounted in a computer-stabilized optical sensor platform (OSP) at the forward end of the TRIM cupola. The OSP could be rotated aft to protect the fragile sensor windows during cats and flights through bad weather. Real-time imagery generated by the

Another view of the NA-6A TRIM development aircraft showing the size of the sensor pods. Operational aircraft would carry a much more refined installation. (Robert F. Dorr Collection)

two optical sensors was displayed on a new multifunction CRT known as the Indicator, Azimuth, Range Multisensor (IARM). A single development aircraft was converted from the same A-6A (BuNo 152914) previously used as an A-6B testbed. Following promising tests with the TRIM OSP at Patuxent River, funds were made available for conversion of a dozen A-6As (BuNos 155647–155648, 155653, 155660, 155662, 155667, 155670, 155674, 155676, 155681, 155684, and 155688) at Grumman Calverton. The first fully-equipped aircraft (BuNo 155647) flew at Calverton on 11 June 1969. The modified aircraft were reaccepted by the Navy between 25 February and 12 June 1970 with a new A-6C designation.

The concept behind TRIM was that there would always be a sensor available to detect a target or OAP. The FLIR or radar could be used at any time, and the LLLTV at dawn and dusk when the FLIR was usually ineffective, or at night in strong moonlight. Typically, the B/N would use the radars to initiate the attack, and the P-7B computer program slaved the optical sensors to the point under radar scrutiny so that the B/N could examine the area in further detail on the IARM. Radar-derived elevation data was then used to compute automatic weapons release.

By the end of April 1970, eight A-6Cs had been delivered to VA-165 for a combat evaluation with CVW-9 aboard the USS *America*. However, four of the A-6Cs were held back at

NAS Whidbey Island for completion of TRIM training and later crossed the Pacific to join the squadron on 18 May. The squadron ended up deploying with five A-6As, eight A-6Cs, and three A-6B PATS. They took fifteen civilian technical representatives, which reportedly outraged the CAG, but each one held a specialty they needed to keep the systems working.

According to Grumman engineers, it took two days to change an engine on the A-6C because the TRIM cupola had to be removed first. When the first Navy technicians arrived at Grumman for training, they quickly tired of dropping the cupola and devised a method of changing engines that did not require removing the TRIM system. This method was subsequently approved by Grumman.

A total of 675 A-6C combat sorties were flown out of a total of 1,058 sorties generated by VA-165 during the course of five line periods between 26 May and 7 November 1970. The LLLTV worked well during the day and under moonlight conditions, and was so sensitive that it could pick up major light sources such as Da Nang Air Base or an aircraft carrier at ranges of up to 50 nm. Unfortunately the Viet Cong did not have large air bases or aircraft carriers, and the LLLTV proved nearly useless for detecting small targets in the adverse weather conditions that prevailed in Laos for most of the combat evaluation.

The FLIR was partially successful in augmenting the radars but had poor resolution and offered a range of only four nm. This was deemed inadequate since in bad weather crews flew at 15,000 feet (nearly three nm in altitude, meaning the FLIR could only detect targets a mile ahead of the aircraft) and only dropped down for the last 15 nm prior to engaging the targets. Only two trucks were sighted by FLIR during the entire combat cruise, mainly due to a fuzzy display and a problem focusing the sensor. Major improvements in FLIR technology were obviously necessary.

On 12 November 1970 five of the VA-165 A-6Cs were transferred to VA-145 aboard USS *Ranger* with three more following a couple of weeks later. VA-145's combat operations, which commenced in the winter months after the monsoon with a large force of 16 Intruders (a 50/50 mix of A-6As and A-6Cs), were able to make much more effective use of TRIM, although damage to the

This photo of the NA-6A (147867) shows the FLIR installation on the side of the fuselage just under the windscreen. The pods on the wings contained the low-light television equipment. (Grumman via the Tony Thornborough Collection)

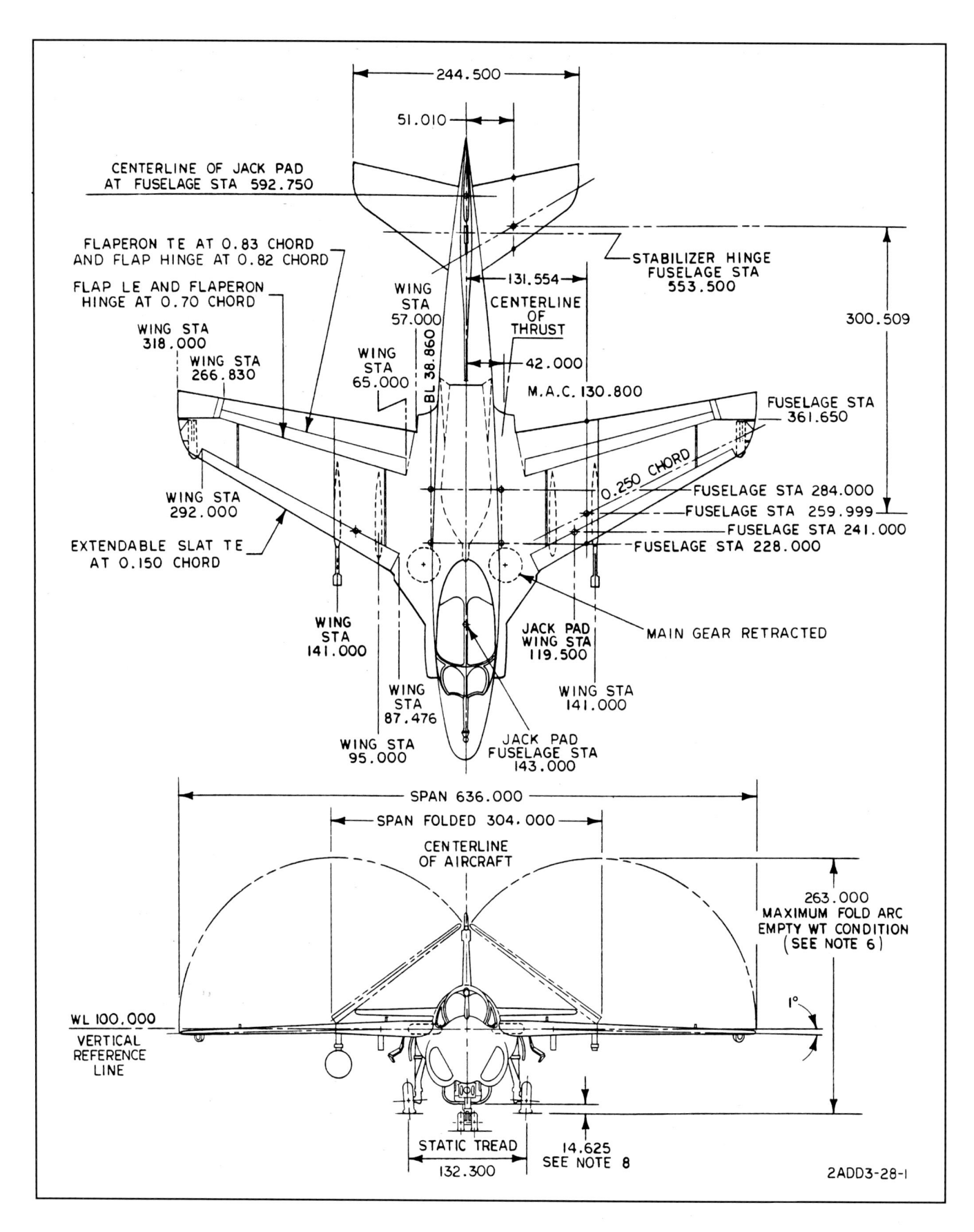

Above and opposite page: The dimensional data for the A-6C (this page and next). In general, the aircraft were externally similar to standard A-6As except for the large TRIM cupola under the centerline. (U.S. Navy)

enemy appeared to remain modest. The cruise, however, was marred by two losses, including CDR Keith Curry's A-6C (BuNo 155647) which was night-catapulted with a full load of weapons only to end up plunging into the water 400 yards in front of the carrier. LCDR Gerald L. Smith, the B/N, was rescued, but search operations failed to find the pilot.

During early 1972 three TRIM A-6Cs had a new laser designator installed in lieu of the LLLTV, and also received upgraded FLIR sensors. These aircraft were assigned to VA-35 for CVW-8's fourth combat cruise aboard the USS *America* in 1972–1973. On 11 August the carrier was stationed off the coast of Vietnam and began launching strike missions into the south, exploring the A-6C as a stabilized laser designator. This technique involved acquiring a target using the radar or FLIR then "illuminating" the target with the laser. Another aircraft, on a similar heading, would drop 500-pound Mk 82 Paveway I bombs fitted with a laser seeker that would guide the bombs into the laser energy reflected from the target. The A-6Cs were also equipped with an ASD-4 direction finder that was intended to find the electromagnetic emissions from truck engines. A similar ASD-5 Black Crow unit equipped AC-130 gunships.

The first successful use of the laser-guided bombs (LGBs) by an A-6C occurred on 5 November 1972, with the second coming on 9 November. Of the thirteen Mk 82 Paveways dropped, seven scored direct hits. A third evaluation strike was scheduled the following week, but demands placed on the A-6's to support LINEBACKER II operations postponed this until 9 January 1973. However, bad weather and a lack of targets resulted in no weapons being dropped.

Follow-on A-6 deployments generally had three TRIM aircraft deployed with each of the three squadrons, VA-34, VA-75, and VA-176, that used the type during its career. By late 1975, the majority of the 11 survivors had their cupolas and associated wiring permanently removed. The A-6Cs were eventually brought up to the latest A-6E configuration while undergoing rework at the Naval Air Rework Facility (NARF) depots or at Grumman Calverton.

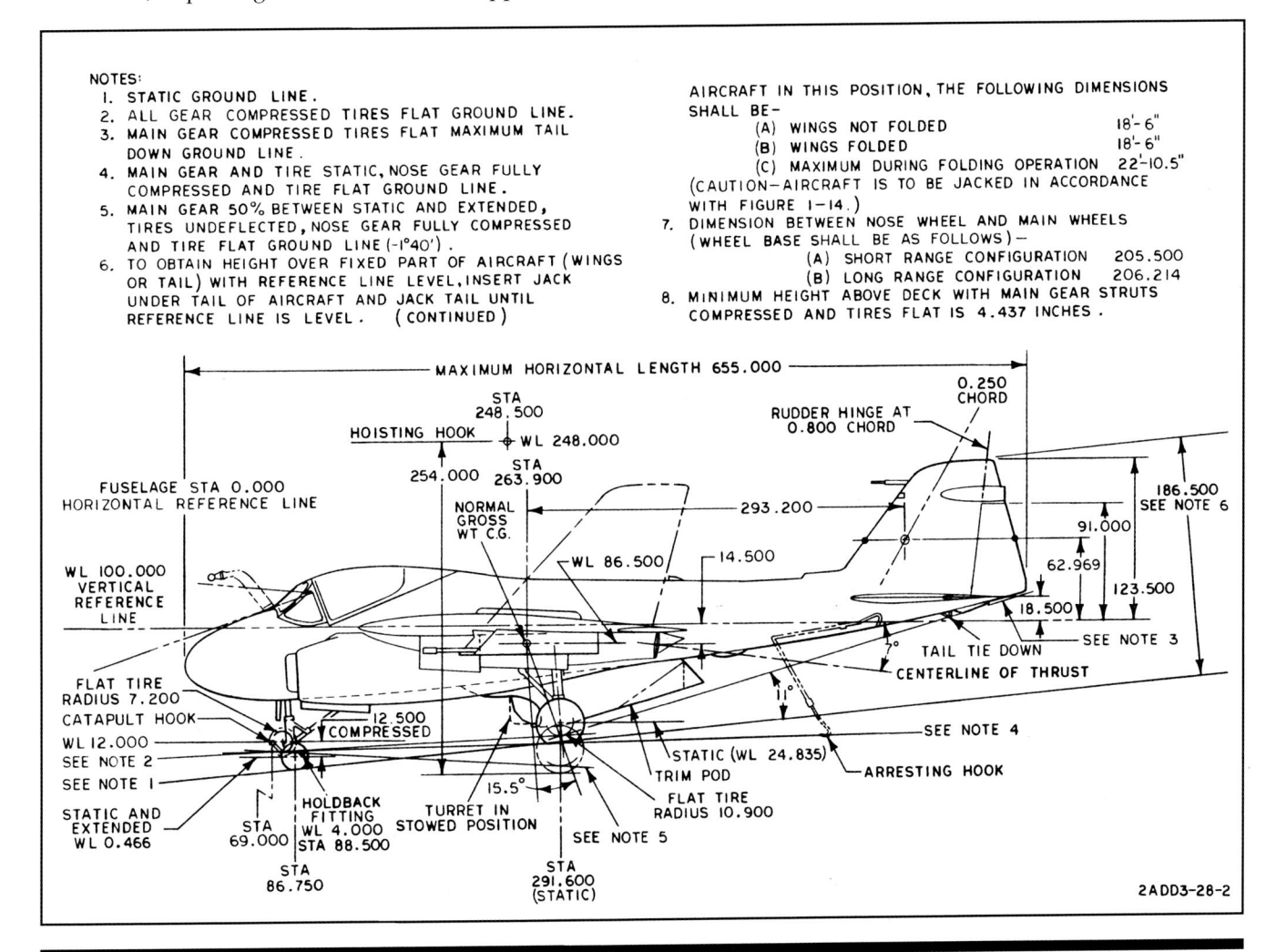

Two nice in-flight views of A-6Cs (155667 above; 155647 below) fresh from modifications at Grumman. The size of the TRIM cupola is evident in these shots. Needless to say, the aircraft could not carry any weapons on the normal centerline station. (Grumman via the Robert F. Dorr Collection)

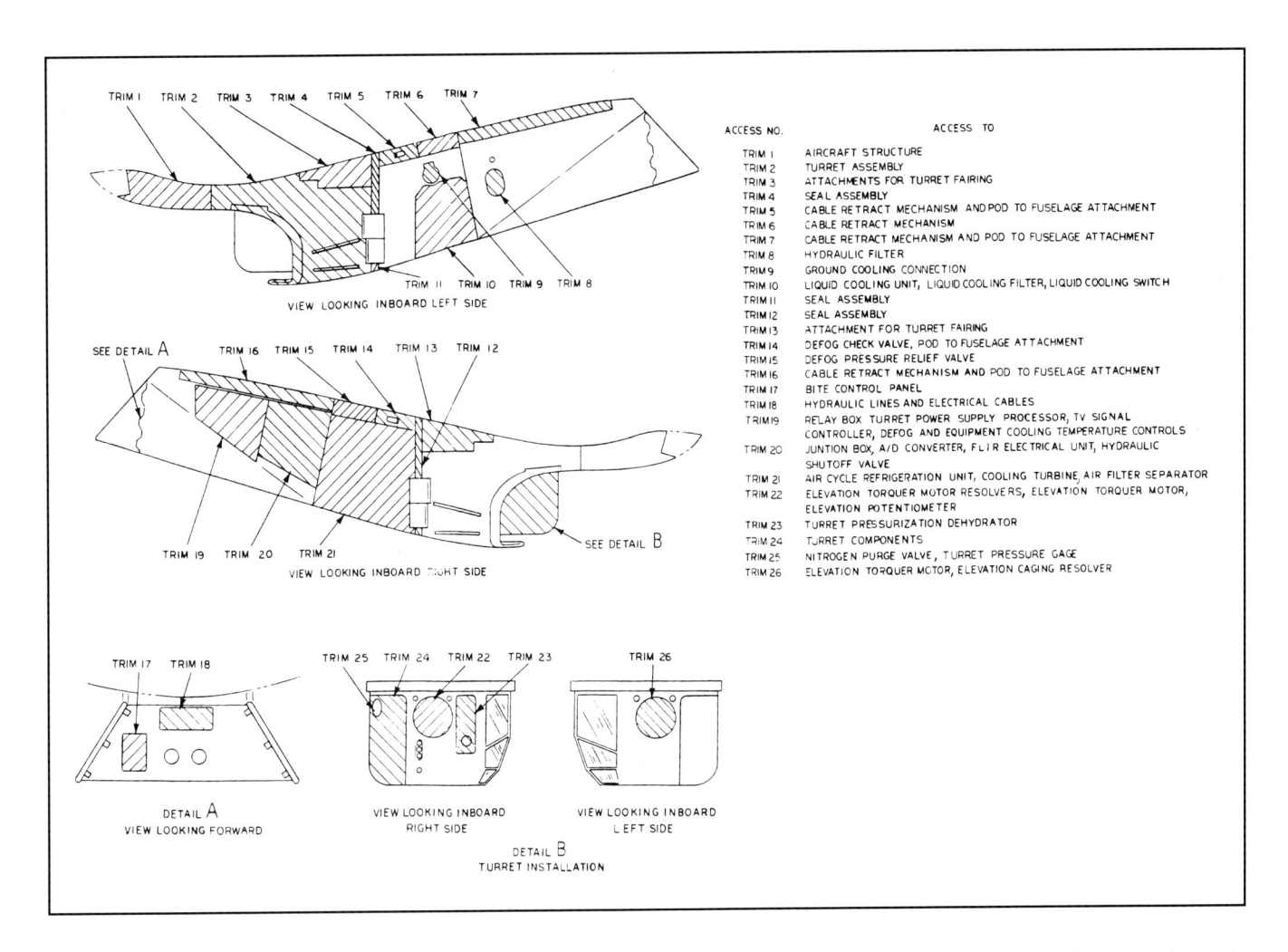

ACCESS NO.	ACCESS TO
TRIM 1	AIRCRAFT STRUCTURE
TRIM 2	TURRET ASSEMBLY
TRIM 3	ATTACHMENTS FOR TURRET FAIRING
TRIM 4	SEAL ASSEMBLY
TRIM 5	CABLE RETRACT MECHANISM AND POD TO FUSELAGE ATTACHMENT
TRIM 6	CABLE RETRACT MECHANISM
TRIM 7	CABLE RETRACT MECHANISM AND POD TO FUSELAGE ATTACHMENT
TRIM 8	HYDRAULIC FILTER
TRIM 9	GROUND COOLING CONNECTION
TRIM 10	LIQUID COOLING UNIT, LIQUID COOLING FILTER, LIQUID COOLING SWITCH
TRIM 11	SEAL ASSEMBLY
TRIM 12	SEAL ASSEMBLY
TRIM 13	ATTACHMENT FOR TURRET FAIRING
TRIM 14	DEFOG CHECK VALVE, POD TO FUSELAGE ATTACHMENT
TRIM 15	DEFOG PRESSURE RELIEF VALVE
TRIM 16	CABLE RETRACT MECHANISM AND POD TO FUSELAGE ATTACHMENT
TRIM 17	BITE CONTROL PANEL
TRIM 18	HYDRAULIC LINES AND ELECTRICAL CABLES
TRIM 19	RELAY BOX TURRET POWER SUPPLY PROCESSOR, TV SIGNAL CONTROLLER, DEFOG AND EQUIPMENT COOLING TEMPERATURE CONTROLS
TRIM 20	JUNTION BOX, A/D CONVERTER, FLIR ELECTRICAL UNIT, HYDRAULIC SHUTOFF VALVE
TRIM 21	AIR CYCLE REFRIGERATION UNIT, COOLING TURBINE, AIR FILTER SEPARATOR
TRIM 22	ELEVATION TORQUER MOTOR RESOLVERS, ELEVATION TORQUER MOTOR, ELEVATION POTENTIOMETER
TRIM 23	TURRET PRESSURIZATION DEHYDRATOR
TRIM 24	TURRET COMPONENTS
TRIM 25	NITROGEN PURGE VALVE, TURRET PRESSURE GAGE
TRIM 26	ELEVATION TORQUER MOTOR, ELEVATION CAGING RESOLVER

Details of the TRIM cupola. The drawing shows the location of most major items, while the photo shows the large aerodynamic fins protruding from the rear of the copula. (above: U.S. Navy; below: Grumman via the Robert F. Dorr Collection)

GRUMMAN A-6 Intruder

47

The new RCA LLLTV and Texas Instruments FLIR sensors were mounted in the computer-stabilized optical sensor platform (OSP) at the forward end of the TRIM cupola. The OSP could be rotated aft to protect the fragile sensor windows during cats and flights through bad weather. The photos at left shows the TRIM turret in its deployed position, exposing the sensor windows. The photos at left and below are of 155647 on a predelivery test flight. (Grumman via the Robert F. Dorr Collection)

The TRIM cupola was a tight fit — it essentially filled the area between the main landing gear, and extended as close to the ground as the Navy believed prudent for carrier operations. However, the unit was fairly streamlined and apparently had little adverse effect on the flight characteristics of the A-6. The turret is shown here in its hidden position. (Grumman via the Tony Thornborough Collection)

Less capable, but much more compact, the Air Force's Ford Aeronutronic-built AVQ-10A PAVE KNIFE pod was modified to be carried on a limited number of A-6s during the early 1970s. (U.S. Navy via Vance Vasquez)

Although not directly related to the A-6C, a similar capability emerged during the latter days in Vietnam as a spin-off from the Air Force PAVE KNIFE project, where a combined laser designator and LLLTV was mounted in a banana-shaped pod that could be carried by a dozen specially wired F-4Ds. The AVQ-10A PAVE KNIFE system was adapted to the A-6 under a $1.777 million contract by Ford Aeronutronic (later Loral), the primary pod contractor. On 18 July 1972 VA-145 was selected for the evaluation, and in October three aircraft were modified with the requisite wire bundles and new cockpit LLLTV display.

VA-145 successfully guided 54 Mk 83 and Mk 84 Paveway laser-guided bombs to their targets during the course of their sixth combat cruise aboard the USS *Ranger* between November 1972 and June 1973. Among other things, these destroyed 14 bridges in North Vietnam. The use of PAVE KNIFE foretold the capabilities of the A-6E TRAM and what would become routine during Operation DESERT STORM, almost two decades later. After the cruise with VA-145, the PAVE KNIFE pods would deploy with several other Navy and Marine A-6 squadrons but never again saw combat.

The AVQ-10A PAVE KNIFE pod installed on an A-6A from VA-145 at the Ford Aeronutronic facility. (Loral via the Tony Thornborough Collection)

This A-6C TRIM aircraft carries a full load of 500-pound Snakeyes under the wings. (Grumman via the Tony Thornborough Collection)

GRUMMAN A-6 INTRUDER

Compared to the A-6C TRIM cupola, the PAVE KNIFE pod was small and fit well on the centerline of the A-6A. (U.S. Navy via Vance Vasquez)

An AVQ-10 PAVE KNIFE pod under one of the VA-145 A-6As at the Ford Aeronutronic facility. Ford performed the modifications to each of the A-6As that were modified to carry the pod. (Loral via the Tony Thornborough Collection)

At least a couple of A-6Es were also modified to carry the PAVE KNIFE pod as this photo of 158041 shows. The aircraft was photographed at NAS North Island. (Mick Roth Collection)

FLYING GAS 4 STATIONS

INTRUDERS AS TANKERS

The jet age presented the Navy with a new problem. Early turbojet engines were notoriously inefficient, and the range of most jet-powered aircraft was unacceptable from an operational perspective. The obvious answer was to exploit in-flight refueling concepts that had been explored as early as 1923. Many A-3s were modified with hose and drogue tanking equipment and became dedicated KA-3 tankers, and the Douglas-developed D704 buddy refueling pack allowed almost any A-4, A-6, or A-7 to act as a tanker. The Navy, however, was not totally satisfied with these solutions since the A-3 had a large deck-space requirement, and using operational attack aircraft as tankers was expensive and reduced the strike force.

KA-6D

As a solution the Navy decided to procure a dedicated tanker based on the Intruder, something first proposed by Grumman in 1965. Company-sponsored trials took place in April and May 1966 using an A-6A (BuNo 149937) equipped with a Sergeant Fletcher hose and drogue refueling kit. A Navy F-4B Phantom II was the guinea pig on the other end of the hose. The results of these tests convinced the Navy that the tanker was exactly what it needed, but it was not until 1969 when the high-priority A-6B/C modifications were completed that the KA-6D tanker variant was finally ordered into production.

Since the new tanker was destined to be flown in a comparatively docile manner, the first batch of 55 KA-6Ds were converted from high-time A-6As. The aircraft nevertheless received a complete airframe refurbishment as part of the conversion process. Four aircraft were modified at Grumman Calverton, with the first (BuNo 151582, shop number K1) making its initial flight on 16 April 1970 with test pilot Chuck Sewell at the controls. The remaining 51 aircraft were modified at Grumman Stuart, in Florida, at a FY70 cost of approximately $860,000 each. The last aircraft from this batch (later known as the Block I configuration) was delivered to the Navy on 14 April 1972.

The initial tankers were equipped with a hose-and-drogue refueling assembly that replaced most of the DIANE components in the mid-fuselage birdcage. With five 300-gallon external tanks, the KA-6D could transfer 2,300 gallons while operating 150 nm from the carrier. Occasionally, a D704 buddy store would be carried on the centerline station as a backup capability in case the primary system failed, but this reduced the fuel available for transfer by 300 gallons since the centerline tank could not be carried. The 55 original KA-6Ds possessed a very limited VFR attack capability, and the Navy reportedly considered mounting a 20mm cannon in the tanker, but this never occurred.

Structurally, the KA-6D was identical to an early A-6A, with the exception of the mid-fuselage birdcage that was modified with the hose-

MAIN DIFFERENCES TABLE

	KA-6D	A-6E	A-6E TRAM
ECM EQUIPMENT	FOR ECM DIFFERENCES REFER TO NAVAIR (01-85ADA-1A)		
ACLS AN/ASW-25 (MODE II)	AFC 230	AFC 230	–
AFT BAY OVERHEAT DETECTION	–	–	x
GENERAL PURPOSE COMPUTER AN/ASQ-133	–	x	–
SEARCH RADAR AN/APQ-148	–	x	–
INERTIAL NAVIGATION SYSTEM AN/ASN-31	–	x	–
VIDEO TAPE RECORDER AN/USH-17(V)	–	x	x
ADDITIONAL AIR CONDITIONING	–	–	x
ACLS (MODE I)	AFC 161	AFC 161	x
RECONFIGURED CNI	AFC 462, 495	–	x
CAINS AN/ASN-92	–	–	x
GENERAL PURPOSE COMPUTER AN/ASQ-155	–	–	x
SEARCH RADAR AN/APQ-156	–	–	x
DRS AN/AAS-33 PROVISIONS	–	–	x
6 VOLT APPROACH LIGHTS	–	–	x
REDESIGNED VDI (IP-722(XJ-1)/AVA-1)	AFC 479	–	* x
ELECTROLUMINESCENT FORMATION LIGHTS	–	–	** x
WEAPONS CONTROL SYSTEM AN/AWG-21	–	AFC 409	*** x

* TRAM AIRCRAFT 160995 AND ON, M215 AND ON
** TRAM AIRCRAFT 161092 AND ON
*** A-6E TRAM 159571, 158796, 159177, 158797, 159579, 158043, 159182, 154140 AND AIRCRAFT INCORPORATING AFC 409

The main differences table from the A-6 NATOPS manual. (U.S. Navy)

and-drogue refueling assembly. The KA-6D differed from other Intruders in being devoid of sophisticated avionics. Almost all displays and controls on the B/N's side of the cockpit were removed, replaced by a minimal number of controls for the refueling equipment. The KA-6D, however, was fitted with chaff dispensers — originally ALE-29 units — then, beginning in mid-1982, with ALE-39s. In mid-1983 the KA-6D also gained an OMEGA navigation system.

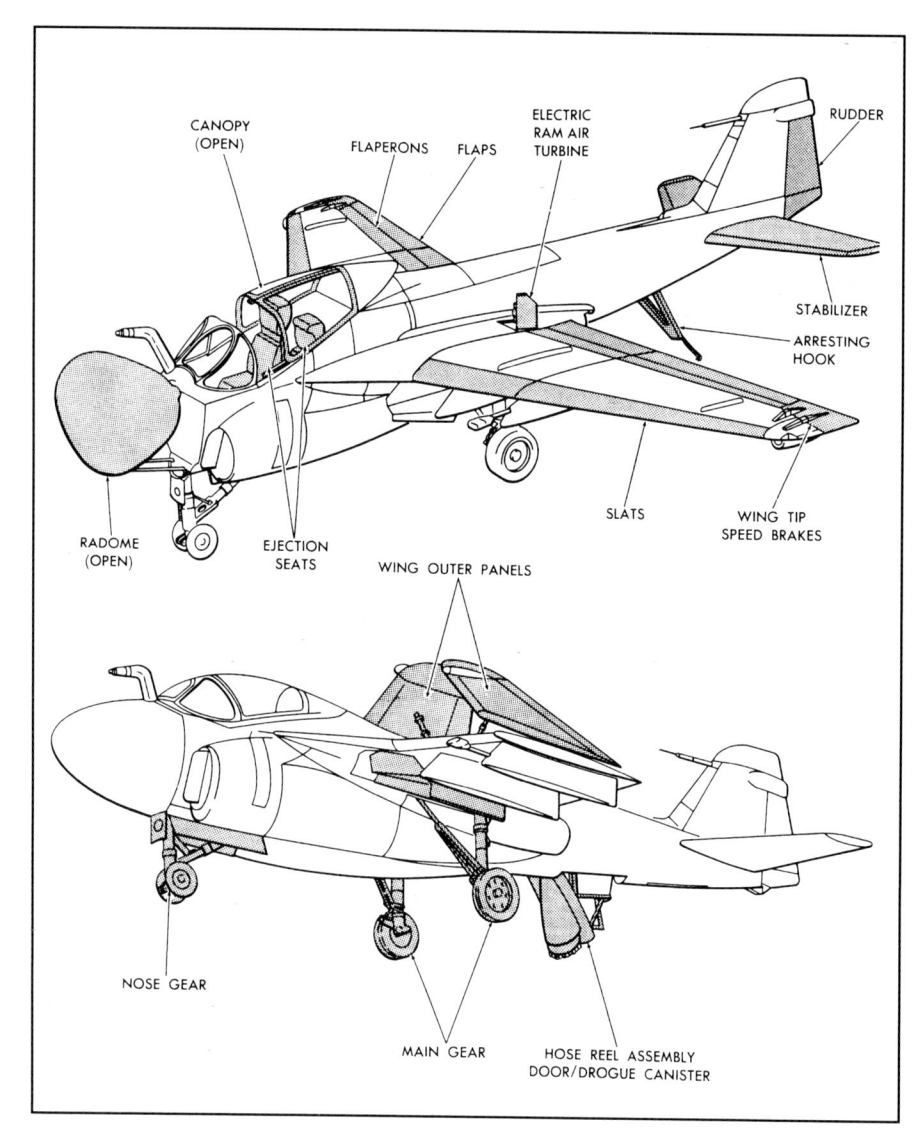

Increased capacity fuel pumps were fitted, raising the normal 150 gallons per minute transfer rate to 350 gallons per minute. A fuel shut-off valve, surge suppression device, and flow meter were also installed. The

A diagram (left) from a service manual showing the major movable surfaces on the KA-6D. The general arrangement diagram below shows the location of most major components inside the aircraft. Note the extensible "bird cage" from the attack variant has been replaced by the hose and reel unit. (U.S. Navy)

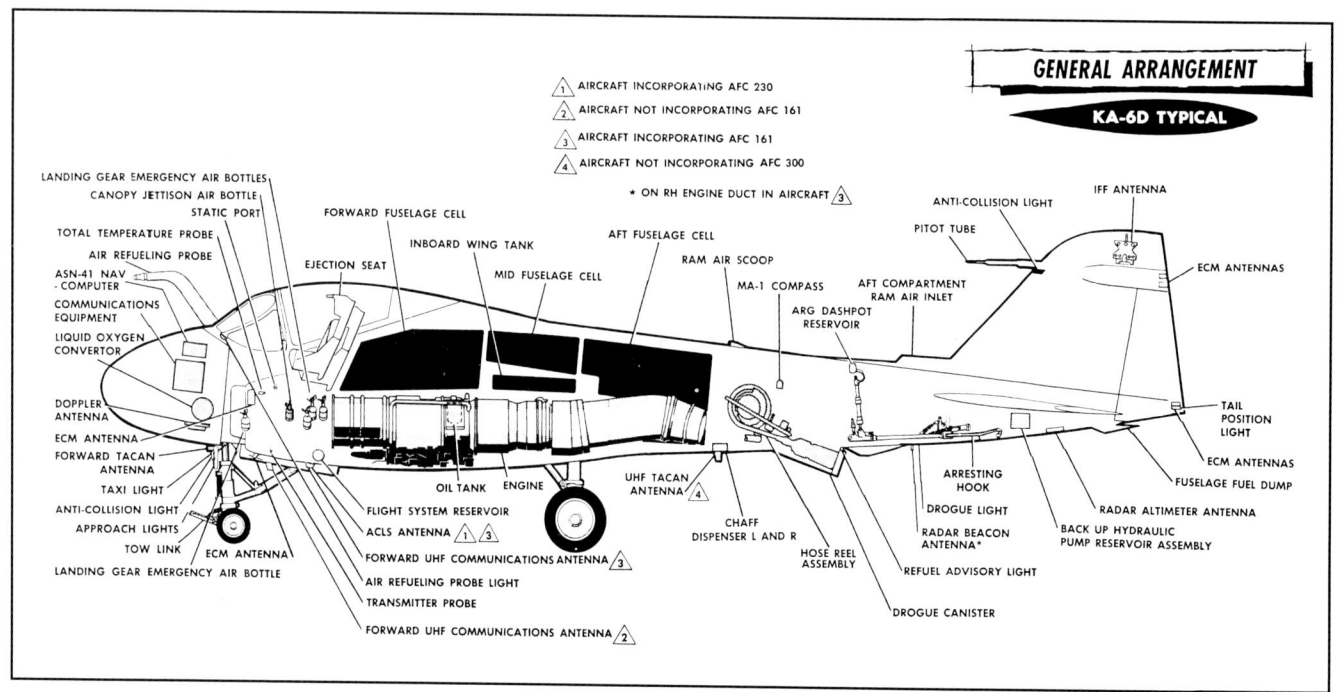

refueling installation contained a drum with 50 feet of 2.375-inch reinforced hose, MA-2 coupling, 26-inch diameter paradrogue, integral night formation lights, pressure regulator, hydraulic motor, and hose guillotine. This self-regulating equipment transferred fuel automatically from the KA-6D on contact with the receiver's probe and could be deployed from 220 to 320 knots IAS.

There were some interesting safety concerns, the most serious relating to a failure of the refueling hose to rewind. This explained the hose guillotine that allowed the crew to sever the hose before attempting a landing. Use of the guillotine (which used explosive charges) was prohibited if a fuel leak was suspected, forcing the crew to seek the safety of a land base if one was available. If it was impractical to return to a shore base, the carrier would generally deploy the emergency barricade in order to recover the KA-6D.

The KA-6D was first deployed in 1971 with VA-85 embarked aboard USS *Forrestal* in the Mediterranean with the 6th Fleet. The squadron was equipped with nine A-6As and four of the new tankers. Even en route to the Mediterranean, the KA-6Ds made a favorable impression by freeing A-6s and A-7s that had been consistently tied up as buddy tankers on previous cruises. The financial savings resulting from the KA-6D were immediate since it cost only $115 per flight hour to operate the KA-6D, compared to $140 for an A-6A. This was due to the decrease in maintenance required between flights, which dropped to 19 MMH/FH, mainly from not maintaining a DIANE system.

During this initial five month deployment, VA-85 made 403 KA-6D

A KA-6D (151821) from VA-165 refuels an A-6A (155595). The KA-6D was much less expensive to operate than a standard A-6 because the DIANE components had been deleted. It also — in theory — kept the attack aircraft available for their primary mission instead of being used as buddy tankers. However, since each squadron traded 3–4 attack variants for an equal number of tankers, in reality the number of available attackers did not materially change. (Grumman via the Tony Thornborough Collection)

sorties totaling 989.5 flight hours, resulting in 3,205 plugs, 1,526 hose cycles, and 3,357,080 pounds of fuel transferred. The KA-6D entered the war in Southeast Asia during the early months of 1971 with VA-176, providing vital support for strikes by Navy and some Air Force aircraft. In the post-Vietnam years the KA-6D maintained its vital role, and it was unusual for a carrier air wing to deploy without at least four tankers aboard.

The Navy ordered a follow-on production run in 1973, converting an additional 24 tankers (shop numbers NK1–24) at the Naval Air Rework Facility in Norfolk using kits supplied by Grumman (actually NK23 had already been converted by Grumman as KA-6D K55, so the NARF rework was therefore a rework of a rework, making a fol-

low-on batch of 23 airframes). The last of these aircraft was redelivered in February 1981. The second batch of KA-6Ds incorporated a few changes, including completely eliminating the visual bombing capability. Although the differences were minor, this batch was divided into three slightly different configurations — Block II (NK1–8), Block III (NK9–16), and Block IV (NK17–24).

During 1978 the Navy instituted a program (AFC 374) to completely replace all of the wiring on the KA-6Ds. This modification was incorporated on the production line during the conversion of the Block IV aircraft. The major impetus behind this program was to create a standard wiring harness that was devoid of the remnants of wiring left behind when the attack systems were deleted. It had appeared that

A CHAFF SAFE PIN AND FLAG SWITCH

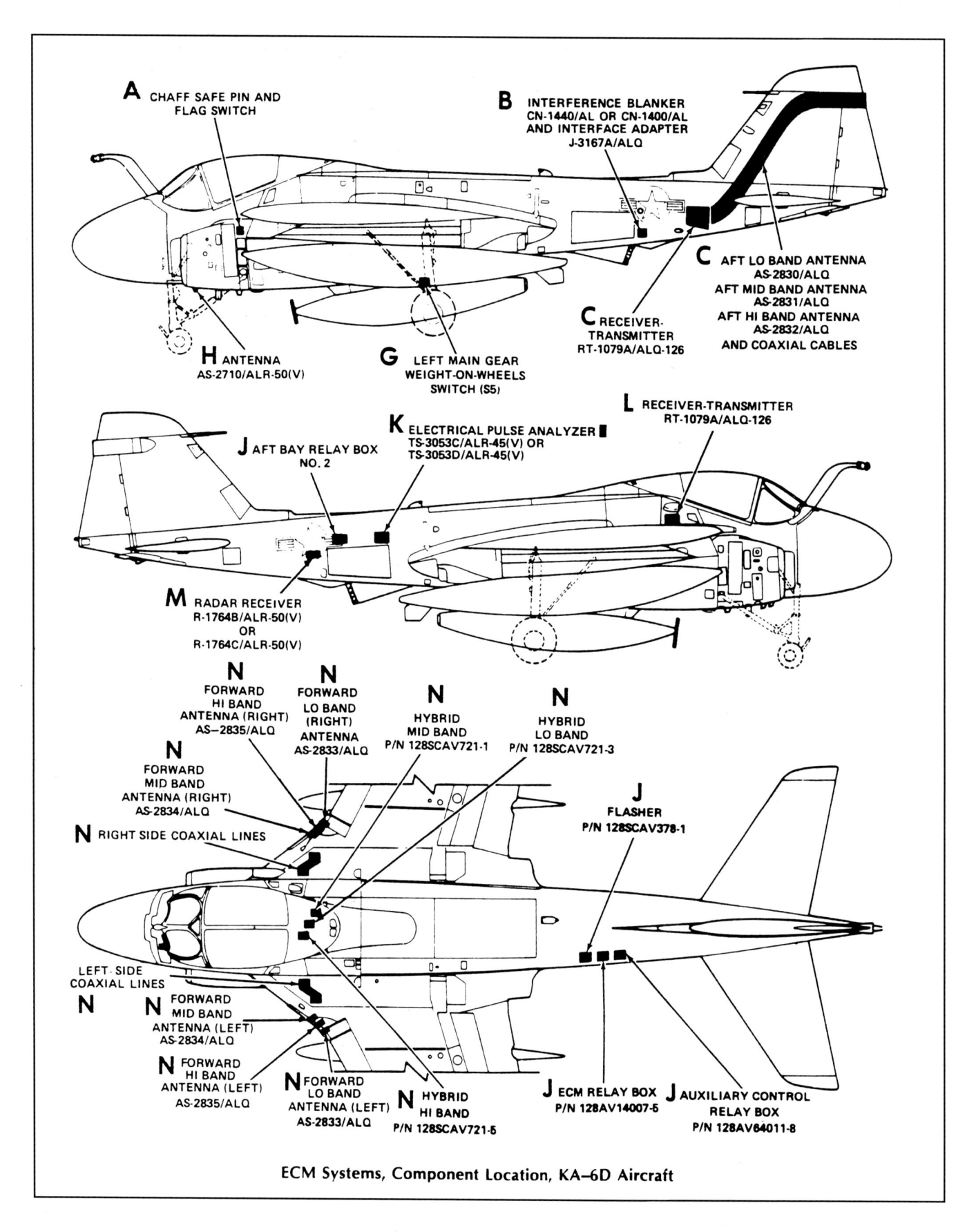

B INTERFERENCE BLANKER CN-1440/AL OR CN-1400/AL AND INTERFACE ADAPTER J-3167A/ALQ

C AFT LO BAND ANTENNA AS-2830/ALQ
AFT MID BAND ANTENNA AS-2831/ALQ
AFT HI BAND ANTENNA AS-2832/ALQ
AND COAXIAL CABLES

C RECEIVER-TRANSMITTER RT-1079A/ALQ-126

H ANTENNA AS-2710/ALR-50(V)

G LEFT MAIN GEAR WEIGHT-ON-WHEELS SWITCH (S5)

L RECEIVER-TRANSMITTER RT-1079A/ALQ-126

J AFT BAY RELAY BOX NO. 2

K ELECTRICAL PULSE ANALYZER TS-3053C/ALR-45(V) OR TS-3053D/ALR-45(V)

M RADAR RECEIVER R-1764B/ALR-50(V) OR R-1764C/ALR-50(V)

N FORWARD HI BAND ANTENNA (RIGHT) AS-2835/ALQ

N FORWARD LO BAND (RIGHT) ANTENNA AS-2833/ALQ

N HYBRID MID BAND P/N 128SCAV721-1

N HYBRID LO BAND P/N 128SCAV721-3

N FORWARD MID BAND ANTENNA (RIGHT) AS-2834/ALQ

N RIGHT SIDE COAXIAL LINES

J FLASHER P/N 128SCAV378-1

LEFT SIDE COAXIAL LINES

N FORWARD MID BAND ANTENNA (LEFT) AS-2834/ALQ

N FORWARD HI BAND ANTENNA (LEFT) AS-2835/ALQ

N FORWARD LO BAND ANTENNA (LEFT) AS-2833/ALQ

N HYBRID HI BAND P/N 128SCAV721-5

J ECM RELAY BOX P/N 128AV14007-5

J AUXILIARY CONTROL RELAY BOX P/N 128AV64011-8

ECM Systems, Component Location, KA–6D Aircraft

Above and opposite page: This diagram and the one on the following page show the location of the major ECM components. (U.S. Navy)

each aircraft was originally converted in slightly different ways, and too much excess wiring remained that was no longer used. AFC 374 cured this situation, and significantly reduced the problems that had been encountered during fleet maintenance. The shop numbers of the rewired aircraft were changed as they went through the modification — Block I became RK1–54 (the original 55th conversion being considered a Block II aircraft), Block II became 2K1–8, Block III became 3K1–8, and Block IV became 4K1–8.

In 1982, Grumman was awarded a contract to convert four A-6Es to KA-6Ds. Eventually, this was expanded to 16 A-6Es — all had begun life as A-6As — converted into tankers and designated the Block V configuration. Eight (MC1–8) were converted by Grumman at St. Augustine, while eight others (KC01–08) were converted by NARF Norfolk using kits provided by Grumman. All of these aircraft had their wiring brought up to AFC 374 standard during the conversion process. This last KA-6D configuration deleted all weapons system

A staged publicity photo of four KA-6Ds trailing their refueling hoses. (U.S. Navy)

capabilities and included provisions to carry five 400-gallon drop tanks. All remaining KA-6Ds were eventually brought up to the Block V configuration, including the deletion of the limited attack capability. A contract for 20 new-build KA-6D tankers (BuNos 158053–158072) was canceled before production began. In the end, a total of 78 A-6As and 16 A-6Es were converted to the tanker configuration.

KA-6H Proposal

During 1976 the Navy conducted evaluations of a KS-3A Viking tanker derived from the Lockheed S-3A antisubmarine aircraft. The KS-3A offered greater fuel capacity than the KA-6D and slightly better tanking qualities since the KA-6D paradrogues had a tendency to swing under certain flight conditions. However, the KS-3 was an expensive airframe, even without the antisubmarine electronics, and it consumed a fair amount of deck space — something already at a premium given the size of the F-14 and other fleet aircraft.

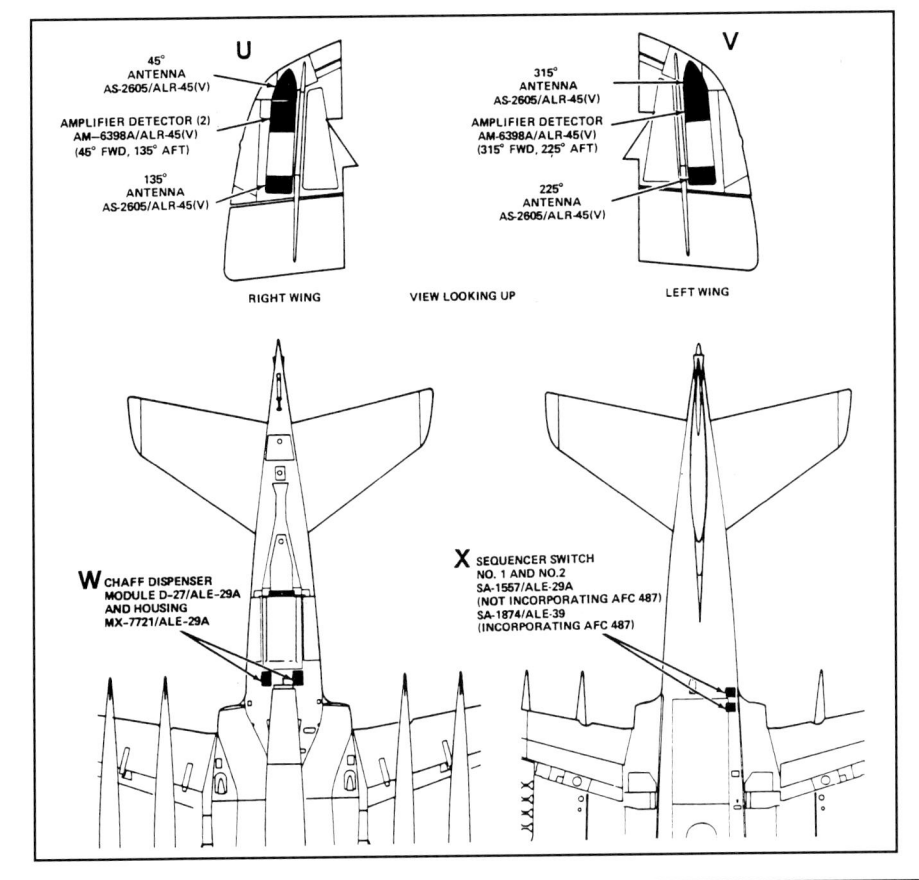

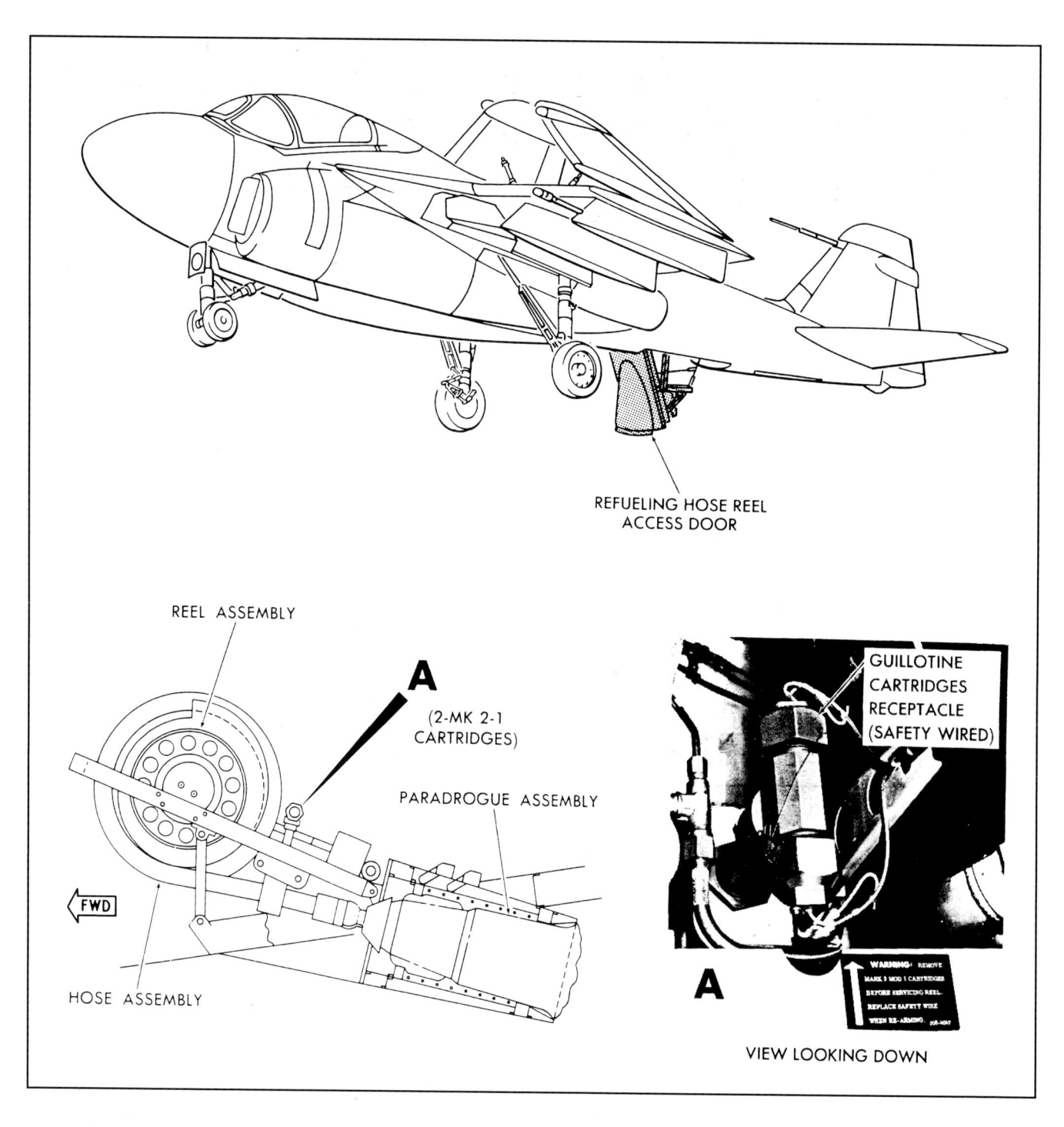

The refueling hose and reel was fitted to the extensible bird cage, just like the electronics on the attack variants. This made servicing and maintenance easier and required the minimum modifications to the basic A-6 airframe. All of the give-away fuel was carried in external tanks, although the internal tanks could be cross-fed if necessary. (U.S. Navy)

In reply, Grumman proposed the KA-6H, a tanker based on the EA-6B Prowler airframe. By adding tanks in place of the rear crew station and in the vertical fin-tip pod, Grumman engineers found room for an extra 6,028 pounds of fuel, resulting in 45 percent more give-away than the KA-6D.

The Navy at one point became seriously interested in the project, and plans were made to convert the fourth preproduction EA-6B (BuNo 156481) into the KA-6H prototype. Forty-two KA-6H aircraft were procured during FY83–85, but in 1979 Defense Secretary Harold Brown announced that he had canceled the program. The proposed prototype was never modified.

A KA-6D (152626) refuels an A-6E TRAM (162180) on 24 February 1988. The difference between the older paint scheme and the newer low-vis gray scheme is well illustrated here. (Robert L. Lawson via the Mick Roth Collection)

This KA-6D (152618) was converted from an A-6A — note the fuselage speed brakes. The wingtip speed brakes are fully open and the trailing edge flaps deployed. The photo was taken on 10 October 1987 at NAS Oceana. (David F. Brown via the Mick Roth Collection)

The external fuel tanks were interchangeable between the KA-6D and the attack variants, so it was not unusual to see different paint schemes on them. This KA-6D (155619) was photographed on 10 October 1987 at NAS Oceana. (David F. Brown via the Mick Roth Collection)

GRUMMAN A-6 INTRUDER

A KA-6D (154103) from VA-35 aboard the USS Nimitz photographed on 20 January 1981. (Robert L. Lawson via the Mick Roth Collection)

VA-34 operated this KA-6D (149940) seen on 10 October 1987 at NAS Oceana. Note the extended tail hook and the built-in stairs to the cockpit. (David F. Brown via the Mick Roth Collection)

Looking a bit worse for the wear, this KA-6D (151792) was assigned to VA-35 aboard the USS Saratoga when photographed in January 1990. (Mick Roth Collection)

This KA-6D (151793) from VA-115 shows a two-tone radome that went a long way toward improving the look of the Intruder. The aircraft was photographed on 9 July 1976 at NAF Atsugi, Japan. (Masumi Wada via the Mick Roth Collection)

By the time this photo was taken on 25 April 1992, the A-6 was on the way out in favor of the A-12. It was less certain what the fate of the KA-6Ds would be, but most everyone assumed they too would pass quickly from service. (Mick Roth Collection)

Like most Intruders during the 1970s, the KA-6Ds carried squadron art work on the vertical stabilizers. Here a KA-6D (151787) shows the markings of VA-52 on 28 November 1977 at NAF Atsugi, Japan. (Masumi Wada via the Mick Roth Collection)

The low-vis gray scheme may have been more effective, but the earlier two-tone white and gray paint made the aircraft look better. This KA-6D (151582) was assigned to VA-34 at NAS Oceana on 11 July 1974. (Jim Tunney via the Mick Roth Collection)

It was not unusual for the KA-6D to carry a buddy refueling pod on the centerline just in case something went wrong with the primary reel system in the fuselage. This reduced the amount of fuel that could be offloaded but allowed a mission to continue in the event of unexpected problems. (Keith Wade via Mark Munzel)

This KA-6D (151789) was photographed at KA-6D Abbotsford, Canada, in August 1990. Note the buddy refueling pod on the centerline. The variation in the two-tone radome makes the nose look a bit more streamlined than it really was. (Keith Wade via Mark Munzel)

The converted A-6As carried the fuselage speedbrakes for their entire careers — it was not worth the money to replace them, so they were left bolted closed. This KA-6D (152893) from VA-115 was photographed on 12 April 1989. (Kevin L. Patrick via the Mick Roth Collection)

GRUMMAN
A-6 INTRUDER

Good detail of the tanker version of the bird cage. In the event the hose would not retract normally, there was a hose guillotine that allowed the crew to sever the hose before attempting a landing. Use of the guillotine (which used explosive charges) was prohibited if a fuel leak was suspected, forcing the crew to seek the safety of a land base if one was available. If it was impractical to return to a shore base, the carrier would generally deploy the emergency barricade in order to recover the KA-6D. (Mick Roth Collection)

Chained to the deck of the USS America, this KA-6D (151579) was assigned to VA-35 in October 1974. Note how far the nose wheel is turned, a necessary attribute to be able to maneuver around the crowded decks of an aircraft carrier. (Mick Roth Collection)

Another converted A-6A tanker (152592), this time assigned to VA-196 during December 1989. KA-6s were often used for cross-country training flights since they cost less per hour to operate than a normal A-6, explaining why the tankers showed up at so many transient bases around the country. The fuselage stripe on this aircraft was typical of most squadrons — a simple vertical stripe around the entire fuselage. (Michael Grove via the Mick Roth Collection)

A shiny recently-refurbished KA-6D (151581) assigned to VA-304 photographed on 23 June 1990. Some squadrons, like this one, were quite elaborate with the stripe around the rear fuselage — others were very simple as seen at the top of the page. It was unusual to see a KA-6 with no external fuel tanks. (Keith Synder via the Mick Roth Collection)

Late in their careers, the KA-6 fleet began getting luminescent formation lighting strips — usually installed across the top of NAVY on the aft fuselage. This KA-6D (151576) from VA-155 had been so equipped when this photo was taken in December 1989. (Michael Grove via the Mick Roth Collection)

VA-304 operated this KA-6D (152921) on 28 March 1993. Note that the refueling basket is not completely retracted into the hose tunnel. (Vance Vasquez via the Mick Roth Collection)

Intruders in Color

Not Always Grey

The intruder was never called beautiful. That description was usually reserved for the "fast movers" — the supersonic fighters like the F-14 Tomcat. But to those that flew and serviced it, the A-6 could not be beat.

Like many U.S. Navy aircraft during the 1960s and 1970s, the A-6 frequently wore colorful squadron markings — especially the "CAG" aircraft. An entire book could be produced showing the schemes used in 30 years of service, but space allows only a few to be presented here.

Many A-6s were also painted in special paint schemes — usually for various tests — during their career. A sample of these are also presented in the photographs that follow.

A few A-6s also received tactical camouflage, although remarkably few color photographs exist of the Vietnam-era experiments, and none are presented here.

Unfortunately, towards the end of its career, almost all A-6s received the standard Navy tactical gray paint scheme, and colorful squadron markings were all but eliminated, The A-6 became boring, like most other United States combat aircraft.

The third A-6A (147866) during December 1973. Note the partially open fuselage speed brake — it is natural metal since it protruded into the engine exhaust when it was extended. A pair of external fuel tanks are on the wing stations and a buddy refueling pod is on the centerline.
(Ron McNeil via the Mick Roth Collection)

An A-6B Mod 1 carries dummy AGM-78 Standard ARMs on the inboard wing pylons. Note the antennas arranged on the forward part of the nose radome.(Grumman via the Robert F. Dorr Collection)

GRUMMAN
A-6 INTRUDER

The A-6E (155673) TRAM test aircraft at Pax River on 21 February 1975. The aircraft was named Super Hunter *by its crews. Note the TRAM emblem on the vertical stabilizer. This aircraft had started life as an A-6A and was later modified to the A-6E configuration. (Ray Leader via the Mick Roth Collection)*

Another A-6A (149940) being used as a test aircraft, this time at NAEC Lakehurst during March 1978. Note that the fuselage speed brakes have been fixed in the closed position and painted to match the rest of the fuselage. (Jim Leslie via the Mick Roth Collection)

A few A-6s received this brown and tan camouflage scheme during the late 1980s. Note that the TRAM turret is still gray, as are the external tanks (which were shared with other aircraft). Photographed in September 1989 at Whidbey Island. (Rick Morgan via the Mick Roth Collection)

66 **WARBIRDTECH SERIES**

One of the more elaborate pieces of A-6 nose art was Puff the Magic Dragon *on an A-6E TRAM (159314) from VA-165. Photographed at Whidbey Island on 27 July 1996. This shot also gives good detail on the air intake and the TRAM turret under the nose. The use of a black leading edge on the intakes was somewhat unusual—more normally they were off-white. (Mark Munzel)*

The TC-4C presented an unusual appearance due to the A-6 radome grafted onto the nose. Under the radome was a standard complement of A-6 radars — the TC-4Cs were eventually upgraded to the same standard as the fleet A-6s. Photographed in July 1976. (Don Logan via the Mick Roth Collection)

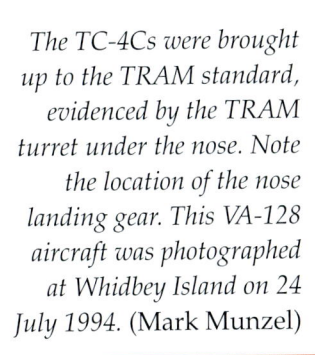

The TC-4Cs were brought up to the TRAM standard, evidenced by the TRAM turret under the nose. Note the location of the nose landing gear. This VA-128 aircraft was photographed at Whidbey Island on 24 July 1994. (Mark Munzel)

GRUMMAN
A-6 INTRUDER

67

An A-6E TRAM cockpit photographed in November 1983. Although not discussed frequently, the A-6 was a nuclear-capable aircraft — the nuclear weapon control panel is just to the right of the word "before" on the tag. (Mick Roth)

A plane director signals to the pilot of an A-6E TRAM on the flight deck of the nuclear-powered aircraft carrier USS Abraham Lincoln (CVN-72) during the ship's shakedown cruise. Note the buddy refueling store on the centerline and the tint to the windshield. (U.S. Navy photo via DVIC)

A pair of A-6E TRAMs from VA-304 on 21 June 1991. The far aircraft (151807) had been built as an A-6A — note the perforated speed brakes on the fuselage. The near aircraft (158531) had been manufactured as an A-6E. (Robert L. Lawson via the Mick Roth Collection)

A KA-6D (152637) from VA-145. This aircraft had been manufactured as an A-6A (note the speed brakes) and converted to a tanker. There is not a stripe around the aft fuselage — a marking that was most always evident during carrier deployments. (Jan Jacobs via the Mick Roth Collection)

One of the A-6Cs shows the large TRIM cupola under the fuselage. The low-light TV and FLIR sensors were mounted in the optical sensor platform (OSP) at the forward end of the TRIM cupola. The OSP could be rotated aft to protect the fragile sensor windows. (Grumman via the Robert F. Dorr Collection)

GRUMMAN A-6 INTRUDER

An A-6E (158795) with General Robert W. Bazley, commander in chief, Pacific Air Forces, aboard waits in line to be launched from the nuclear-powered aircraft carrier USS Carl Vinson (CVN-70). Bazley was departing after a visit to the ship. This shot also shows the difference between the older paint scheme (aircraft in back) with the low-vis gray scheme. The EA-6B in the upper left corner shows the extended forward fuselage. (U.S. Navy photo via DVIC)

An A-6E TRAM from VA-128 is enveloped by steam on the flight deck of the USS Ranger following the launch of another aircraft. The A-6's theoretical replacement — the Boeing (McDonnell Douglas at the time) F/A-18 Hornet is shown at the left of the photo. In reality, the Hornet made a poor replacement for the A-6 due to range and payload limitations. (U.S. Navy photo via DVIC)

A flight deck crew member signals to the pilot of an A-6E TRAM as the aircraft is readied for launch from the USS Coral Sea. The different color shirts on each of the deck crew denotes a different job function — the colors provide ready identification during intense periods. (U.S. Navy photo via DVIC)

A pair of A-6Es show one of the colorful markings used during the early part of the Intruder's career. Note the slight variation in the CAG marking (far aircraft) — it was not unusual for the CAG to have radically more colorful markings, although that is not the case here. (Mick Roth Collection)

This KA-6D (152911) from VA-115 was photographed on 1 April 1975 at NAF Atsugi, Japan. Note the green stripe around the aft fuselage at the base of the vertical stabilizer — most KA-6s had a stripe here to differentiate them from attack A-6s. Typical of the period, even the drop tanks are painted in the squadron colors. (Masumi Wada via the Mick Roth Collection)

When the A-6 got boring, this was the result — two-tone dull gray wraparound camouflage. This A-6E TRAM (159311) from VA-35 was photographed at NAS Oceana on 10 October 1987. The interior of the leading edge devices, wingtip speed brakes, and trailing edge flaps were all painted bright red. (David F. Brown via the Mick Roth Collection)

GRUMMAN
A-6 INTRUDER

The second A-6F (162184) in the Grumman anechoic chamber shows an AIM-9 Sidewinder and an AGM-88 HARM missile under the wing. The A-6F would have provided the Navy with a substantial increase in attack capability, but was cancelled in favor of the A-12. (Grumman via the Robert F. Dorr Collection

After the A-6F program was cancelled, the third prototype (162185) was used as the digital systems development (DSD) prototype for the proposed lower-cost A-6G variant. Unfortunately, it was not to be, and no actual A-6Gs ever flew. (Grumman via the Robert F. Dorr Collection

An A-6E (159567) assigned to the Strike Aircraft Test section of the Naval Air Test Center photographed at NAS Oceana on 29 April 1977. Note the extended equipment rack under the aft fuselage. (Ray Leader via the Mick Roth Collection)

INTRUDERS GET BETTER

1970s HIGH TECH

While the A-6A demonstrated outstanding qualities as an all-weather attack aircraft, the DIANE weapons and navigation systems were based on technology from the mid to late 1950s. This was evident in the amount of maintenance required by the system to keep it operational and the increasing difficulty in obtaining some spare parts. The resulting low readiness rates, particularly aboard carriers where the environmental conditions were less than ideal, were compounded by the long logistics tail back to the United States.

Partial or total failures of DIANE were experienced by as many as 60 percent of the combat sorties flown over Southeast Asia during the late 1960s. Nevertheless, in spite of its 1950s-era avionics, the A-6A represented the best all-weather strike aircraft in the fleet. Even if the system worked only 40 percent of the time, that was far better than any of the competition. The A-4 and A-7 pilots liked to remark that they could put bombs directly on target using their highly-reliable "iron sights," but neglected to mention that this was only under ideal visual conditions. When weather closed in, or at night, the A-4 and A-7 were nearly useless. The Intruder remained the only all-weather attack aircraft available to Naval Aviation. Still, advances in technology during the late 1960s led Grumman and the Navy to believe a significantly improved Intruder could be built.

A-6E

The new Design 128S was formally proposed to the Navy in July 1967 and authority to proceed was given in December 1969 under the A-6E

An A-6E (161107) from VA-165 on the USS Constellation *configured as a buddy tanker on 2 June 1981. Although the KA-6D was widely available, sometimes attack A-6s still performed as tankers using a centerline buddy refueling pod and four drop tanks under the wings. (Robert L. Lawson via the Mick Roth Collection)*

A typical CVW-9 strike force from the USS Constellation, *shown from the B/N's seat of an A-6E on 29 November 1974. A group of LTV A-7 Corsair IIs is at top left, led by a McDonnell Douglas F-4 Phantom II. Immediately ahead of the A-6 is an EA-6B Prowler electronic warfare aircraft, with several other A-6s around it.* (Naval Historical Center)

An A-6E (155632) from VA-36 comes to a halt after making an arrested landing on the flight deck of the nuclear-powered aircraft carrier USS Abraham Lincoln *during the ship's shakedown cruise. Note the open wingtip speed brakes and the deflection on the arresting hook as it snags the cable.* (U.S. Navy via DVIC)

designation. Contrary to most upgrades, the 128S did not significantly advance the capabilities of the A-6A, but instead was intended to significantly reduce the amount of maintenance required by increasing the reliability of the aircraft's avionics. The 128S design contained three major modifications — a new solid-state IBM ASQ-133 general purpose computer to replace the old mechanical drum-based unit, a single Norden APQ-148 multimode radar package to replace the twin search and tracking radar installation, and the substitution of a modern armament control panel for the obsolescent distributed armament control equipment originally installed. These changes reduced the number of black boxes by 17 and their overall weight by 568 pounds.

The A-6E prototype was a modified A-6A (BuNo 155673) that made its maiden flight on 27 February 1970 with Grumman project pilot Joe Burke and B/N Jim Johnson at the controls. The uneventful flight from Grumman Calverton lasted 1.5 hours, but the aircraft only contained the new computer and armament system — the development of the APQ-148 was taking longer than expected. The aircraft was externally identical to the A-6A and used the same J52-P-8A engines that had been used on late A-6As. The new APQ-148 radar became available not long after this flight, and was included on all production aircraft.

The APQ-148 could perform three functions simultaneously — search, track, and terrain clearance. It could detect small ships from a range of 30 nm at 200-foot altitude and targets as small as submarine snorkels at lesser ranges. A new interferometer eliminated the need for the separate radar units that were previously used to compute elevation and range data. The installation of the APQ-148, coupled with the new ASQ-133 computer, resulted in a bombing accuracy nearly twice as good as that of the A-6A. Maintainability was improved by the extensive use of built-in test equipment and reliability was improved through the use of more solid-state components.

Although the Navy was impressed with the capabilities of the A-6E, there was very little money available for new procurements. In order to meet all fleet requirements within a constrained budget, the Navy adopted a two-tiered approach in acquiring the A-6E. A total of 94 new-production aircraft would be built at a rate of approximately 12 per year through FY77 and an additional 240 A-6As would be converted in lieu of procurement (CILOP) to the A-6E standard at a rate of 36 per year. As the war in Vietnam dragged on, this plan was later changed to include 318 new-production aircraft, and still later to 346 aircraft. Not all A-6Es, as it turned out, were exactly the same — there were about a dozen minor differences ranging from the instrument panel to dive brakes — but all possessed similar capabilities.

In 1972 Grumman was awarded a contract for the long-lead items needed to begin the CILOP conversions. The CILOP process significantly reduced the cost of the new A-6E fleet — in FY76 the cost of a new A-6E was estimated at $9.5 million, while converting an A-6A cost only $1.6 million. This margin diminished over time as newer, more expensive systems were introduced into later A-6E configurations, but nevertheless, the CILOP A-6E remained a bargain right up until the last delivery in March 1980.

An A-6E launches two AGM-123 Skipper rocket-powered laser-guided bombs. These weapons were technically not missiles, but rather standard GBU-16 (modified Mk 83) 1,000-pound LGBs that had an 8 x 25-inch rocket motor from a Shrike missile added to the back in order to extend their standoff range. (Emerson Electric via the Tony Thornborough Collection)

This Skipper was displayed at the Point Mugu air show. (Mick Roth)

A-6As slated for CILOP were withdrawn from operational squadrons as they became due for major overhauls. Each aircraft was flown to the NARF depot in Norfolk where it underwent base-level maintenance prior to being sent to Grumman Calverton for modification. At Grumman, each aircraft was thoroughly inspected and early A-6As were brought up to the structural standard used on later A-6As and the new A-6E. The converted aircraft were then processed down the same

TURNING RADIUS AND GROUND CLEARANCE

56° NOSE GEAR DEFLECTION

- WINGS EXTENDED 38' 4"
- STABILIZER 35'
- WINGS FOLDED 23' 6"
- NOSE 26' 5"
- NOSE GEAR 21'
- MAIN GEAR 17'
- PIVOT POINT
- MAIN GEAR 6'

Front view dimensions: 21' 11", 16' 2", 4', 7' 10"

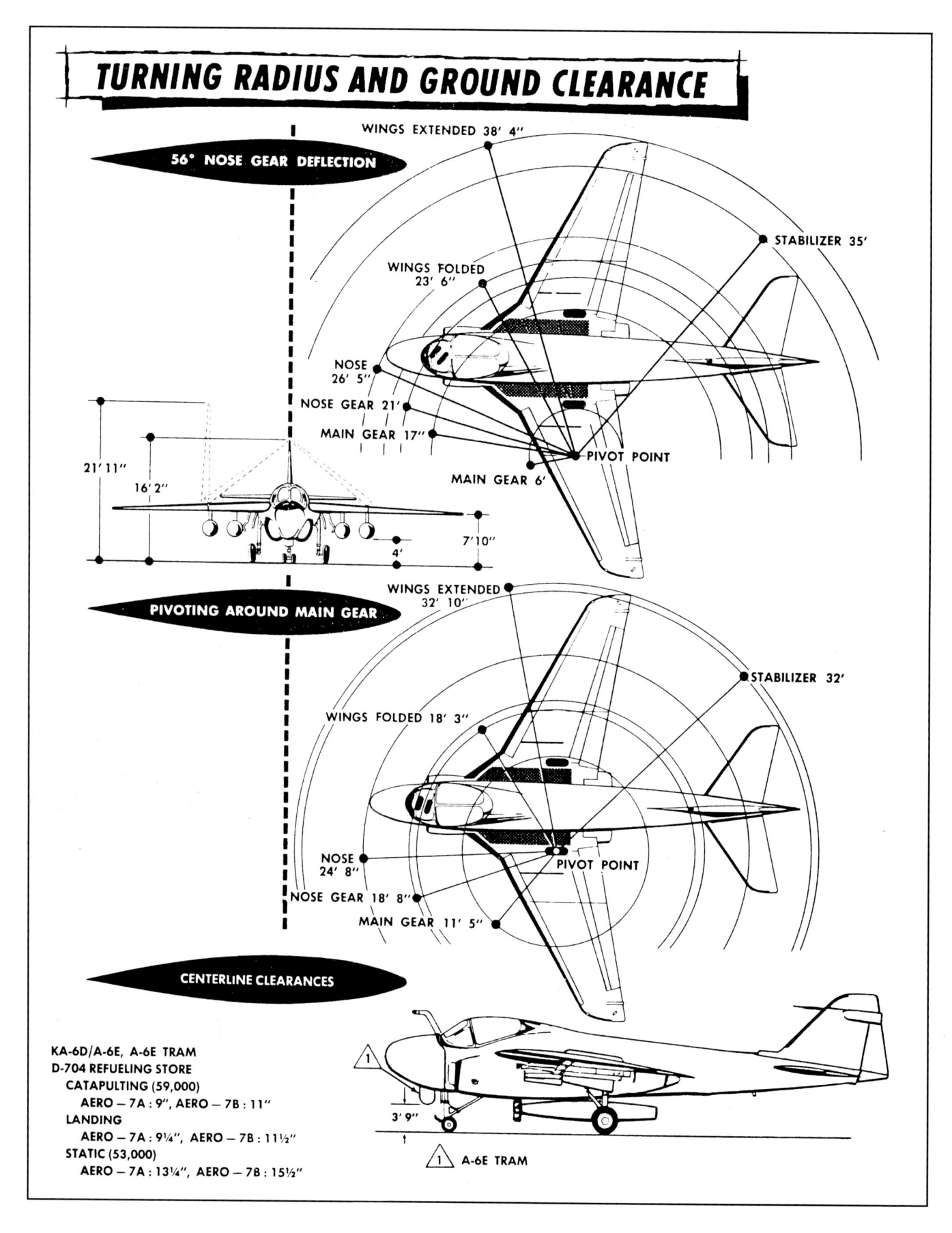

PIVOTING AROUND MAIN GEAR

- WINGS EXTENDED 32' 10"
- STABILIZER 32'
- WINGS FOLDED 18' 3"
- NOSE 24' 8"
- NOSE GEAR 18' 8"
- MAIN GEAR 11' 5"
- PIVOT POINT

CENTERLINE CLEARANCES

KA-6D/A-6E, A-6E TRAM
D-704 REFUELING STORE
  CATAPULTING (59,000)
    AERO – 7A : 9", AERO – 7B : 11"
  LANDING
    AERO – 7A : 9¼", AERO – 7B : 11½"
  STATIC (53,000)
    AERO – 7A : 13¼", AERO – 7B : 15½"

[1] 3' 9" — A-6E TRAM

The turning radius diagram from the NATOPS manual also provides some basic dimensional data for the A-6E. (U.S. Navy)

WARBIRD TECH SERIES

production lines in Plants 6 and 7 as the new-production aircraft. The only post-modification external indications that an airframe began life as an early A-6A were the speedbrakes on the aft fuselage — it was decided that the speedbrakes did not represent a potential corrosion problem, and they were simply bolted in the closed position with their actuators and associated plumbing removed. The CILOP aircraft carried Grumman shop numbers beginning with "M" (for modification) and would later be known as A-6E "mods."

The first new-production A-6E (BuNo 158048, shop No. E-8) was accepted by the Navy during a ceremony on 17 September 1971. Initial A-6Es were assigned to VA-42 for training duties. VA-85 was the first operational squadron to receive the new aircraft, on 9 December 1971. The first operational flight occurred six days later.

The first CILOP A-6E (BuNo 152907, shop No. M-1) emerged on 16 April 1973. Grumman was facing hard times, and by the summer of 1973 the production lines were running behind schedule. This situation was largely brought about by financial woes concerning the F-14A Tomcat that were threatening to bankrupt the corporation. This had obvious psychological repercussions on the work force, affecting both quality control and delivery schedules.

The Navy had expected to take delivery of 36 CILOP A-6Es and 12 new-production aircraft, along with 12 EA-6Bs, during calendar year 1973. However, by the end of Spring the outlook was bleak for even half that number being completed. In an effort to solve this problem the final assembly process in Plant 6 was completely reorganized. The A-6 assembly process was originally centered around a trestle structure that had been installed to facilitate comfortable shoulder-level assembly work.

However, subsequent changes to the New York fire regulations had forced Grumman to raise the structure about two feet, making it extremely uncomfortable to work at. The trestle accommodated six aircraft and all were supposed to be completed at the same time so that they could be simultaneously conveyed down the line. In reality, all six were seldom ready at the same time, so workers were chasing unfinished jobs around the assembly area, and sometimes even into the systems shop in Plant 7. Grumman discarded the trestle concept, and final assembly was restructured with the aircraft on fixed jigs parked in echelon. This meant that a delay with one aircraft would not hold up the assembly line and that no aircraft had to be moved before it was completed.

By the end of the year production and rework rates were catching up, with new-build E-36s being delivered on 5 December and CILOP M-36 on 17 December, just in time to meet the 1973 deadline. Grumman workers had painted "Merry Christmas Navy" on the vertical stabilizer to celebrate the minor victory.

By mid-1974 Grumman was on the road to financial recovery, and the various assembly lines were beginning to return to their normal efficiencies. That year saw 64 A-6s roll out of Calverton, including 18 new-production A-6Es, 40 CILOP A-6Es, and 6 EA-6Bs. This production rate was sustained in 1975, when 58 A-6Es were handed over. A-6 production had been expected to end in late 1976, but the Navy awarded new contracts for A-6Es and EA-6Bs that would extend this date significantly. By the end of 1985 a total of 162 A-6E new-production aircraft had been delivered.

The Grumman manufacturing facilities late during A-6 production. Note that A-6s, EA-6Bs, and F-14s are intermixed on this portion of the line. (Grumman)

The A-6 air intake was large enough for a man to climb into, and several videos exist of crewmen being sucked into the intakes accidentally during ground power runs — fortunately without serious injury. Here a squadron maintenance crewman inspects an engine intake as part of a preflight check of a VA-34 A-6E on the flight deck of the USS Dwight D. Eisenhower *during FLEET EX '90.* (U.S. Navy via DVIC)

An A-6E without a TRAM turret sits on the deck of the USS Enterprise *on 19 December 1996. Note the AGM-88 High-speed Antiradiation Missile (HARM) on the inboard wing pylon. This aircraft had been painted up in "traditional" colors for the last cruise of the Intruder.* (Robert F. Dorr)

A-6E CAINS

In the late 1970s, the original A-6E gave way to the A-6E CAINS (carrier airborne inertial navigation system) configuration that introduced the Litton ASN-92 inertial navigation system in place of the ASN-31 system used on earlier A-6Es. The A-6E CAINS aircraft had an additional air scoop on top of the fuselage near the vertical stabilizer, this fed a new air-conditioning unit that provided more cooling for the electronics. The ASN-92 was significantly more accurate and faster to align than its predecessor while offering improved reliability and commonality with the F-14, E-2C, and S-3. Prior to take-off, CAINS was aligned by using a data-link to interface to the ship's inertial navigation system.

To aid the pilot during carrier landings, particularly at night or in bad weather, an ASW-16 automatic flight control system was coupled to the CAINS approach power compensator to provide fully automatic "hands off" carrier landing capability.

A-6E TRAM

The moderately successful combat evaluation of A-6C TRIM aircraft in 1970 demonstrated the potential of using advanced imaging devices on fast attack aircraft. However, it was realized that these early sensors were very primitive, and this resulted in both the Air Force and Navy sponsoring a great deal of research in the immediate post-Vietnam period. The resulting technology appeared to offer significant improvements over the comparatively crude systems that had been installed on the A-6C.

TRAM was introduced into the A-6E in 1976. The TRAM incorporated a

Hughes AAS-33 detection and ranging set (DRS) consisting of a laser designator, laser rangefinder, and infrared sensor mounted in a 20-inch diameter turret that protruded from the bottom of the fuselage just forward of the nose wheel. The system occupied space that originally held parts of the second radar that had been used on the A-6A. The turret was gyro-stabilized with the laser systems co-linearly mounted on the FLIR to ensure boresight of the laser with the FLIR. The turret's stabilization and pointing system provided full 360-degree lower-hemispheric coverage and could be slaved to the radar. The laser also had a receiver capable of detecting targets illuminated by a ground observer or another aircraft. Later TRAM aircraft had a Northrop infrared video automatic tracking (IRVAT) system that largely automated the tracking portion of the TRAM system.

The FLIR had a continuous 5:1 optical zoom, automatic focusing, and magnifications up to 13X. Temperature differences as small as one degree Fahrenheit could be detected by the FLIR, and data was displayed on a CRT mounted above the B/N's radar scope. A video tape recorder already installed in the A-6E provided a viable bomb damage assessment capability. Using the TRAM systems, the A-6 crew was able to view relatively poor television-quality images of their targets day or night, greatly improving both ballistic and visual bombing accuracy. Other avionics were also significantly upgraded on the TRAM aircraft. The APQ-148 multimode radar was replaced by an improved APQ-156 and a new IBM ASQ-155 digital computer with the ability to provide target data to fire-and-forget missiles. New dual UHF radios, an APX-72 IFF set, and an ARC-84 TACAN were also installed.

A series of shots showing a VA-165 A-6E lowering its wings as it prepares for launch from the USS Nimitz. *(Brian J Plescia)*

GRUMMAN A-6 INTRUDER

The TRAM development aircraft (BuNo 155673) made its first flight on 22 March 1974 at Grumman Calverton. Enough of the system was installed by October that fully integrated tests could begin, although it was not until 29 November 1978 that an A-6E (BuNo 160995) first flew in the complete TRAM configuration. Nevertheless, the system came together much quicker and smoother than the systems on the A-6A — the Navy and Grumman had learned from previous mistakes. The first fleet aircraft to roll out of Grumman with full TRAM capability was an A-6E (BuNo 155710) "mod" (i.e., an A-6A that had been brought up to the A-6E configuration) that was delivered on 1 December 1978, followed by the first new-build A-6E TRAM on the 14th. The first squadron to operate A-6E TRAMs was VA-165 deployed on board the USS *Constellation* in January 1977.

There were three ways an A-6E could be equipped with TRAM. The first was called a production TRAM, and logically enough was an A-6E that was equipped with TRAM on the production line (many of these aircraft were "mods" — A-6As that were converted to A-6Es — but had TRAM installed at the same time). The TRAM Backfits (TBs) were aircraft that were equipped with the wiring and structural provisions for TRAM on the production line (either new-builds or "mods"), but had the actual TRAM system installed at some later date. The TRAM Retrofits (TRs) were A-6Es that were initially delivered with no provisions for TRAM and were subsequently modified in a single step. Interestingly, new-build A-6Es were intermixed in TR and TB configurations, even after TRAMs began rolling off the line. Initially, 32 aircraft were converted to A-6E TRAM configuration (the number subsequently increased to 228) and the A-6E TRAM eventually became the standard for the fleet. Part way through the TRAM program, a "multiple missile capability" was provided that added a missile switching unit with provisions for carrying HARMs (high-speed anti-radiation missiles) and Harpoon, Walleye, and Maverick missiles.

The FY86 cost for a new-production A-6E TRAM, based on a production run of 11 aircraft annually, was estimated at $32.6 million — 10 years earlier the cost had been $18.3 million ($9.5 million in FY76 dollars). A good deal of the cost increase was brought about by additional equipment installed on late A-6Es, including the ASN-92 CAINS (approximately $1 million) and TRAM ($3.2 million). The remaining difference largely represented the cost of a low production rate (11 per year versus the earlier 48).

Considering when it was developed, the A-6 was a marvel of automation. The B/N could preset up to four targets (or three-way points and the target) into the computer, and the VDI showed a target symbol for each. The pilot kept the steering symbol superimposed on the target

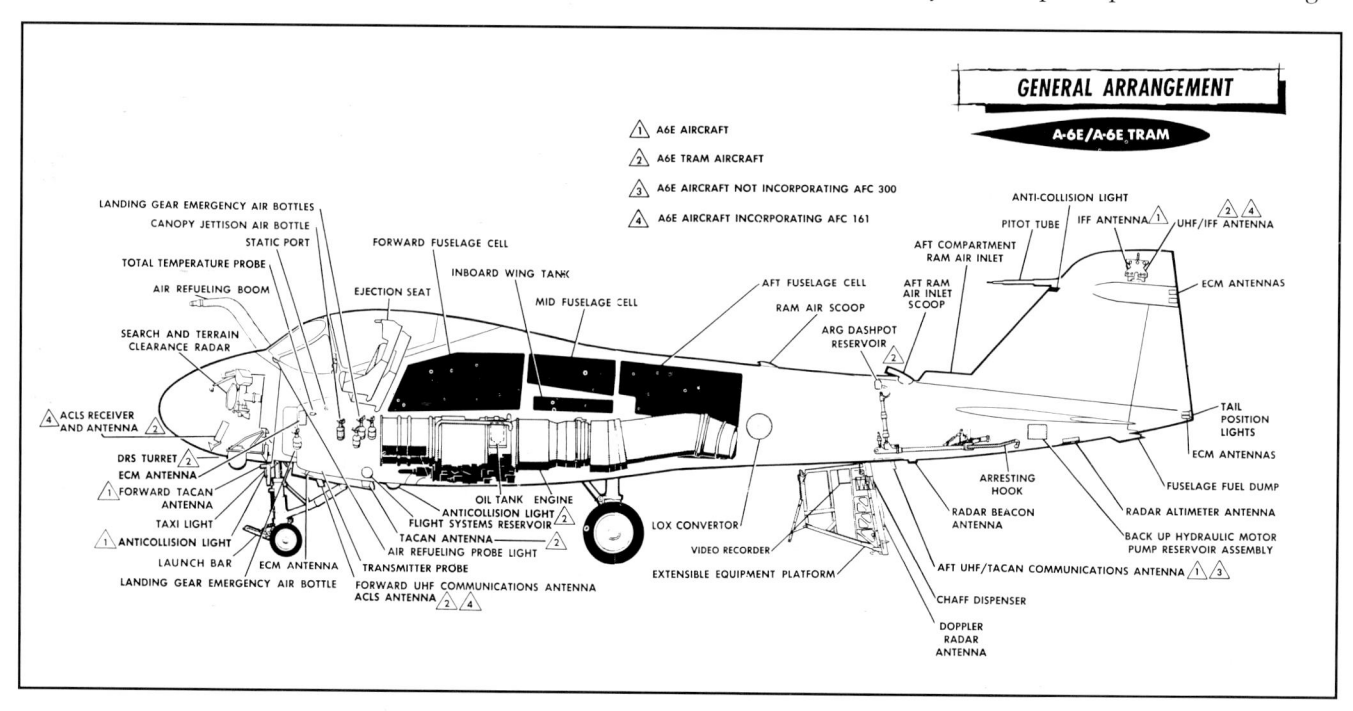

The general arrangement diagram from the A-6E NATOPS manual. (U.S. Navy)

symbol to stay on track. An IN RANGE light illuminated when 10 seconds from the target. In the meantime, the B/N selected the desired bomb rack combination for the attack and either SALVO (one rapidly-sequenced drop) or TRAIN release for the weapons. The latter could be programmed on the ordnance intervalometer so that one bomb (usually the fourth of six) landed directly on the target while the rest straddled it. During weapons release the pilot held the aircraft steady for about 20 seconds at the exact altitude, speed, and dive angle called for on the VDI. Immediately after weapons release the VDI displayed the probable distance by which the bombs missed the target based on the amount of evasive action taken during the run-in.

The A-6E TRAM took this procedure one step farther by integrating the FLIR and laser to further enhance bombing accuracy. Since the radar, VDI, and TRAM sensors were all integrated, the FLIR could be slewed onto target based on radar tracking or stored target coordinates. The FLIR could also be used to differentiate between decoys and real targets by indicating the amount of heat in an object. A "dark" target, such as an inflatable or wood decoy, indicated no residual heat, while a "light" target could indicate that the object was (or had recently been) active.

Slewing the FLIR based on radar or stored coordinates enabled the B/N to go directly to the telescopic narrow field-of-view for detailed optical tracking, while the DRS slew position could be used by the computer to make minor steering corrections on the VDI. It was also possible to operate the FLIR in a manual mode, using its wide field-of-view for target search, then switching

A trio of A-6E TRAMs from VA-128 on 26 February 1988. Each aircraft has a load of 500-pound Snakeye bombs under the wing. (Robert L. Lawson via the Mick Roth Collection)

Outward visibility — at least to the front and sides — was excellent thanks to a large canopy and the innovative arrangement of the pilot's seat slightly higher and ahead of the B/N's seat. (Brian J Plescia)

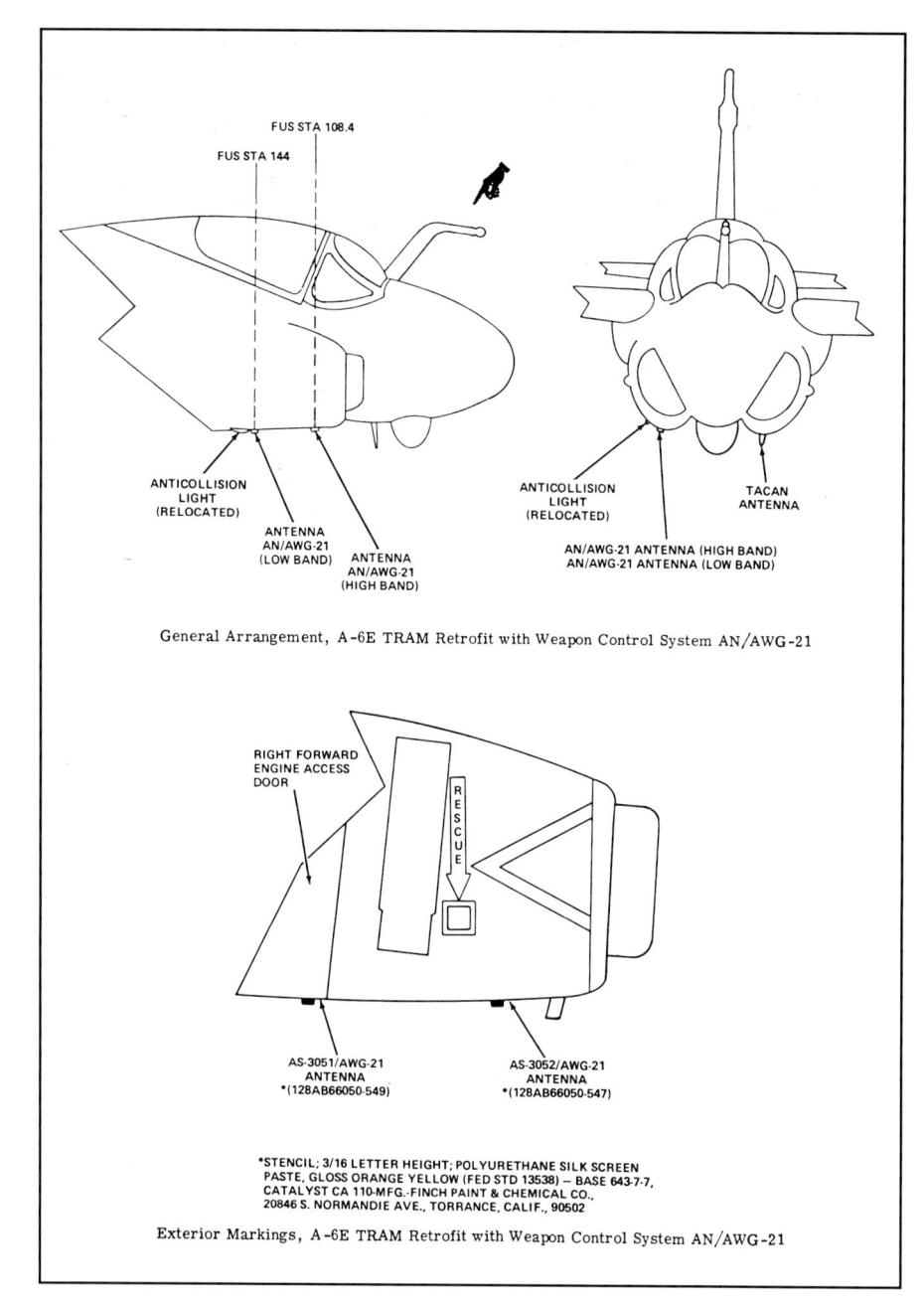

General Arrangement, A-6E TRAM Retrofit with Weapon Control System AN/AWG-21

Exterior Markings, A-6E TRAM Retrofit with Weapon Control System AN/AWG-21

A diagram showing the arrangement of the antennas for the AWG-21 system installed on the A-6 to improve the targeting for Standard ARM. (U.S. Navy)

over to the narrow field-of-view when something interesting appeared on the display. This was generally not considered optimal since the FLIR and its display had a relatively poor resolution, making target identification difficult, especially at high speeds.

The laser designator/ranging system was fitted behind the small left porthole on the DRS turret and was boresighted with the FLIR. The laser could be used to determine the slant-range to target, in lieu of radar, with an accuracy of ±5 feet. This was useful when the A-6 did not want to announce its presence by emitting high-powered radar signals. Using these inputs, the attack computer could provide circular error probabilities of approximately 30 feet.

The laser designator could also be used to autonomously mark a target for an LGB. Alternately, troops or forward air controllers could mark the targets using their laser designators. The laser receiver was behind the starboard porthole on the DRS turret and lased targets were plotted on the FLIR display as a small square symbol. This information could also be used as a reference for non-LGB attack by slewing the DRS so that the FLIR crosshairs were superimposed over the square symbol. Radar or laser slant-range could then be used for bomb delivery without the crew ever having seen the target.

The FLIR could also be used to update the navigation system, and the pilot could use FLIR imagery on the VDI to assist with low-level navigation by showing obstacles such as power lines or radio antennas that were not readily apparent on the radar-provided VDI imagery. Late in the TRAM's career Northrop developed an automatic infrared video tracking system, IRVAT, that enabled the onboard computer to keep track of a target on the FLIR display with only minor assistance from the B/N.

A-6E/AWG-21

During the late 1960s, it had become obvious that although the Standard ARM was a significant improvement over the earlier Shrike, a better anti-SAM missile was still needed. Development of the Texas Instruments AGM-88 HARM began in 1969, although Shrike would continue to be used as late as Operation DESERT STORM in 1991.

Pending the development of HARM, the Navy modified 10 A-6Es (151593, 151782, 151812, 152929, 155588, 158539, 158792, 158795, 159185, and 159574) under AFC 409 issued on 1 July 1978 by incorporating the NAFI AWG-21 fire control processor to improve its Standard ARM capability. A further eight aircraft (154140, 158043, 158796, 158797, 159177, 159182, 159571, and 159579) were subsequently modified during the early 1980s. The second batch all consisted of TRAM retrofit aircraft, and the survivors from the first batch were later put through the TRAM program. What is not clear is whether the first batch retained the AWG-21 system after the TRAM conversion — documentation would seem to indicate not.

The AWG-21 was an attempt to provide more accurate targeting data for the existing AGM-78 Standard ARM. The new system provided the capability to automatically detect, identify, and display ground threat emitters arranged in order of priority. The AWG-21 was designed around a high-speed (for the day) CV-3228 minicomputer plus various hardware-based logic circuits. The computer ran software that contained a reference list of all known emitters (frequency, pulse-repetition rate, etc.) and could compare detected signals against this list and display up to three targets to the B/N.

The only changes to the exterior of the aircraft were the relocation of the anticollision light on the right forward engine door and the addition of two small AWG-21 antennas — a low-band antenna on the right forward engine access door at fuselage station 144 and a high-band antenna on the lower forward area of the right engine air inlet duct at station 108. The AWG-21 provided a much-needed improvement, but by 1987 the Navy had discovered that most Standard ARMs had developed cracks in the solid-fuel rocket motors. Since HARM was entering

Like all Navy aircraft, the A-6 could also be refueled using Air Force tankers and a special adapter that allowed the normal flying boom system to interface with the probe-and-drogue system used by the Navy. (Mick Roth Collection)

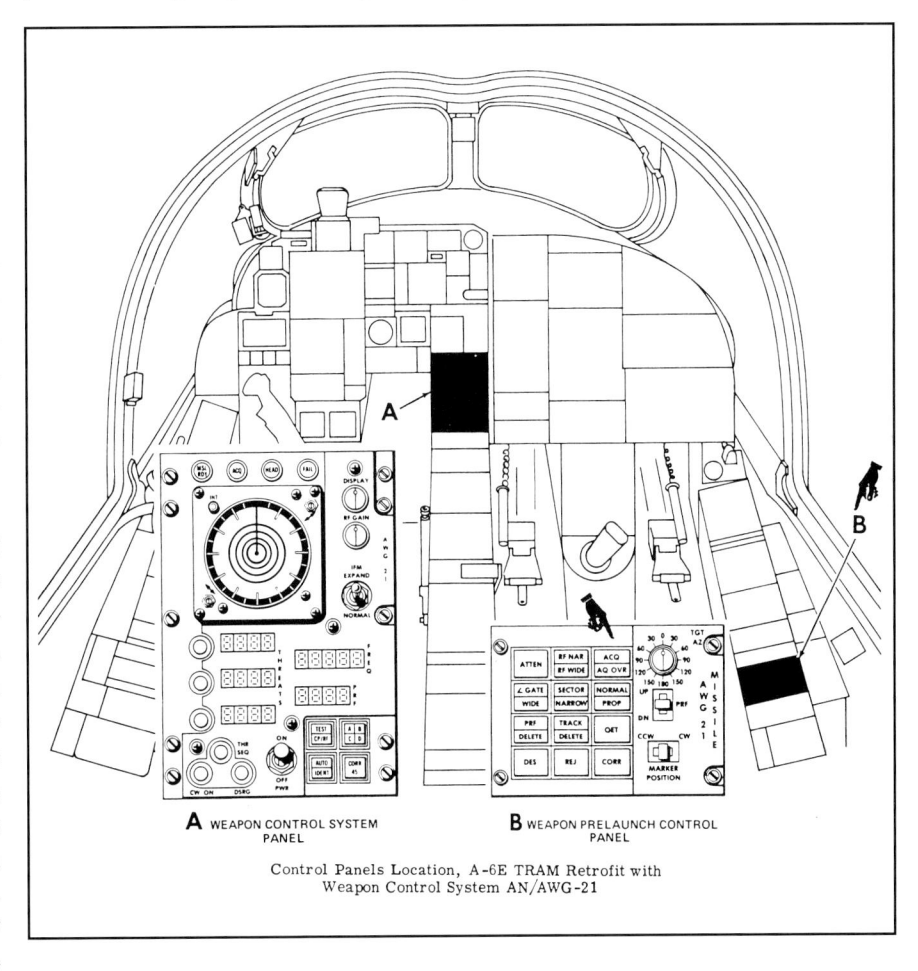

The AWG-21 was an attempt to provide more accurate targeting data for the AGM-78 Standard ARM. The modification added two small panels in the cockpit of the A-6, and changed the function of several displays. (U.S. Navy)

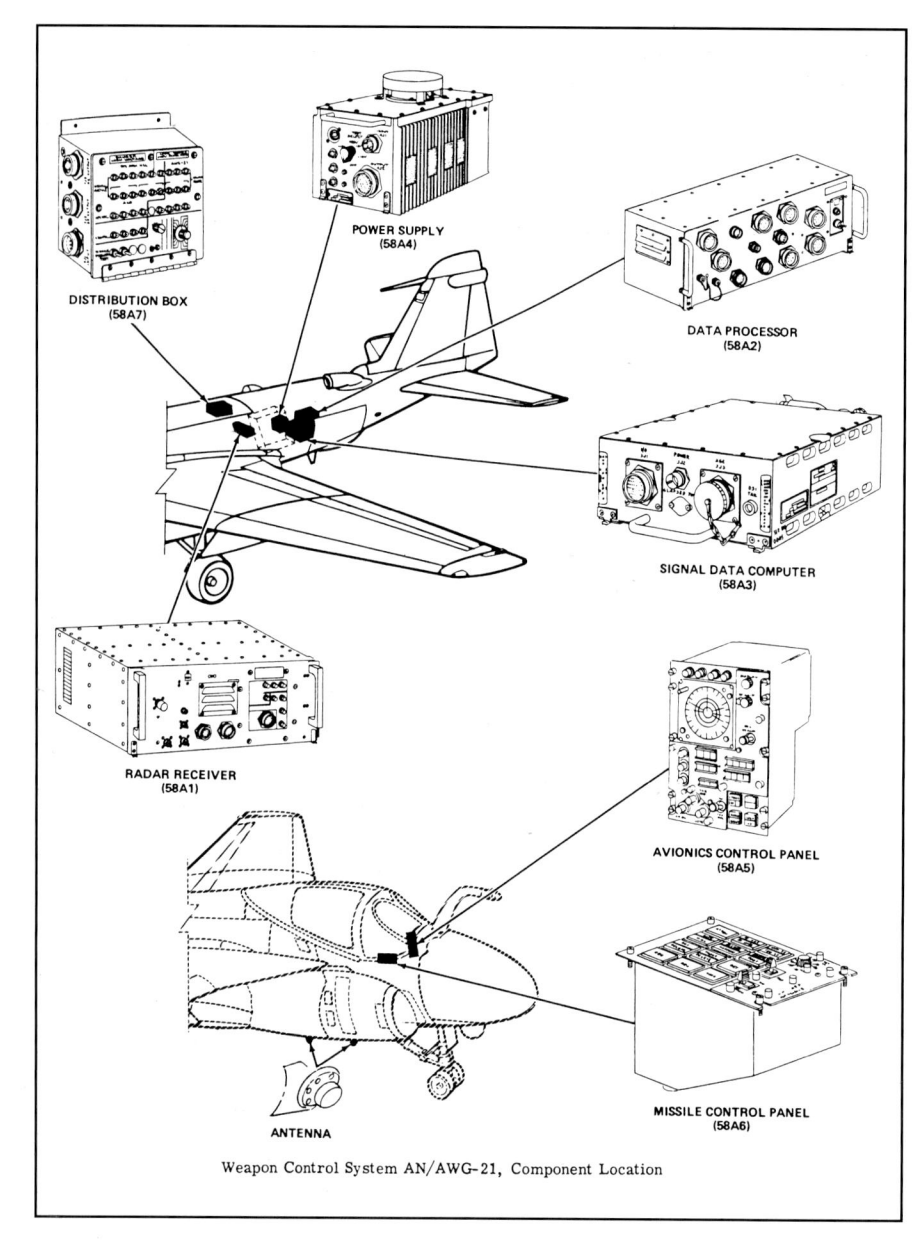

Weapon Control System AN/AWG-21, Component Location

A variety of new "black boxes" were added as part of the AWG-21 upgrade. Although the upgrade was deemed successful, the Navy decided to retire the Standard ARM in favor of the newer AGM-88 HARM. (U.S. Navy)

service the Navy decided to retire the Standard ARM instead of replacing the motors.

A-6E SWIP

The System Weapons Improvements Program (SWIP) for the A-6E TRAM provided additional software that allowed the use of new weapons such as the AGM-65E/F Maverick, AGM-84A Harpoon, AGM-84E SLAMs, and the ADM-141 Tactical Air-Launched Decoy. The SWIP upgrade also included survivability improvements such as an improved fire warning and extinguishing system. To take full advantage of the new weapons, a fully digital armament system along with new weapons displays and controls was also provided. The first SWIP aircraft were delivered to operational squadrons in early 1990.

NEW WING

By the end of 1984 it was becoming clear that the strains of carrier life, and in many cases combat, were taking their toll on the Intruder's wing structure. The original wing had been designed for a 4,500-hour service life, but Grumman and the Navy had underestimated the strains that would be put on the aircraft during low-level operations, and the actual fatigue life appeared closer to 2,500 hours. As early as 1968 Grumman had investigated fitting the 6,000-hour wing designed for the heavier EA-6B to the entire A-6 family. VA-165 had suffered a six-day grounding in 1970 due to wing cracks, and several squadrons had aircraft undergoing wing repairs by 1973.

At first the problems had seemed isolated, but during the early 1980s the Navy instituted a program to rebuild the wings on selected airframes as a means of increasing service life. This initial rewinging program was carried out by Grumman at its Calverton and St. Augustine plants. Accelerometer readings from individual aircraft were used to select candidate airframes for the rewinging program. By the end of 1985 a total of 68 aircraft had passed through the rewing process.

By this time it had become clear that the problem was not isolated to a few airframes. In 1985 cracks and corrosion were discovered in 176 A-6Es and 11 KA-6Ds, all of which were grounded while temporary repairs were made. A better solution would obviously need to be found if the A-6 was destined to continue in service. Grumman still maintained that fitting the EA-6B wing was the fastest and most cost-effective solution, but the Navy was hesitant since the Prowler wing had not been designed for low-level attack missions. Grumman also investigated "load alleviation" techniques, using the wing-tip airbrakes to automatically damp out gust-induced bending loads on the wing, and although this would have provided a minor amount of relief, it did not solve the root problem.

In early 1985 the Navy announced that it had decided to compete a contract for a new wing design. Grumman and the Boeing Military Airplane Company in Wichita were the only two bidders. Boeing was selected in May 1985 based primarily on cost and schedule factors, although the proposed technical implementation differed considerably from the one proposed by Grumman. While Grumman had wanted to use a traditional all-metal (primarily aluminum) wing that was essentially a slightly stronger version of the one used on the EA-6B, Boeing elected to push the state-of-the-art and proposed a mostly-composite structure. This, in theory, promised to end the corrosion problem once and for all, and also to provide a much stronger structure with no weight gain — important given that the A-6 was constantly getting heavier because of the increased avionics being installed on it.

The new wing was constructed primarily from graphite-epoxy composite material, with some titanium used in high-stress areas (such as the wing-fold) and aluminum control surfaces. The first of five initial qualification wings was completed in 1987 and test-flown at Pax River later that year. The new wings had a rocky start — the first wind tunnel test in late 1986 resulted in the full-scale model being destroyed. By January 1988, components of the first production wings were being assembled in Wichita but, when the two pieces were bolted together, the composite material began coming apart around the bolts. The problem required considerable reengineering and the entire rewinging effort was delayed by 28 months. Ultimately, Boeing produced a workable design that met all the requirements established by the Navy.

Boeing provided an 8,800-hour warranty for the wings, and total costs were expected to be $1,200 million for 336 sets of wings, although this was overcome by events and only about half that number were actually manufactured. Two airframe changes were issued on 1 November 1989 to install the new wing in existing aircraft — AFC 592 ("Incorporation of GFE Wing and Fatigue Tolerant Bulkheads in A-6E TRAM Aircraft [ECP 921]") and AFC 599 ("Replacement Wing, Aircraft Kit Configuration Changes for Installation with Replacement Wing [ECP 921R2]").

An A-6E TRAM without the nose turret installed (note the blank plate covering the area that should house the turret). Also note the kill marks under the canopy. (Robert F. Dorr Collection)

Squadron Service — The Navy and Marines' Finest

The A-6A entered service in March 1963 with the Atlantic coast replacement air group, VA-42. Less than two years later the initial operational squadron, VA-75, took the Intruder into combat over Vietnam from the USS *Independence*, on 1 July 1965 — VA-85 was next, flying from the USS *Kitty Hawk*. When the East Coast squadrons deployed to the Pacific and Vietnam, they temporarily wore tail codes beginning with "N" instead of their usual "A." The Marines also took the A-6A to Vietnam, and like the Navy, met with considerable success. A-6A squadrons made 33 combat deployments to Vietnam from nine different aircraft carriers. The Intruder earned an unmatched reputation with both Naval Aviators and the ground troops they supported, but a total of 51 A-6s were lost during the conflict. Eventually, 263 would be lost to all causes (combat, training, operational mishaps, etc.).

Twenty-three U.S. Navy squadrons flew the Intruder, including: VA-34 (A-6A/B/C/E, KA-6D), VA-35 (A-6A/B/C/E, KA-6D), VA-36 (A-6E), VA-42 (A-6A/B/C/E, KA-6D, TC-4C), VA-52 (A-6A/B/E, KA-6D), VA-55 (A-6E, KA-6D), VA-65 ((A-6A/B/E, KA-6D), VA-75 (A-6A/B/E, KA-6D), VA-85 (A-6A/E, KA-6D), VA-95 (A-6A/E, KA-6D), VA-115 (A-6A/B/E, KA-6D), VA-128 (A-6A/E, TC-4C), VA-145 (A-6A/B/C/E, KA-6D), VA-155 (A-6E, KA-6D), VA-165 (A-6A/B/C/E, KA-6D), VA-176 (A-6A/C/E, KA-6D), VA-185 (A-6E, KA-6D), VA-196 (A-6A/B/E, KA-6D), VA-205 (A-6E, KA-6D), VA-304 (A-6E, KA-6D), VAH-123 (A-6A), VAQ-129 (A-6A), and VX-5 (A-6A/B/E, KA-6D).

During a span of 29 years in Marine Corps service, the A-6 was flown by six combat squadrons and a dedicated training squadron. These squadrons flew combat missions in Southeast Asia, and also in Southwest Asia, some 20 years apart. All of the squadrons that made up the Marine A-6 program had their beginning at MCAS Cherry Point, North Carolina. VMA(AW)-242 was the first, and after being established as an A-6 squadron at Cherry Point, moved temporarily to NAS Oceana to train with VA-42. Following 242 (A-6A/E) was VMA(AW)-533 (A-6A/E, KA-6D), VMA(AW)-224 (A-6A/E, KA-6D), VMA(AW)-225 (A-6A), VMA(AW)-121 (A-6A/E, KA-6D), and VMA(AW)-332 (A-6A/E). Eventually, VMAT(AW)-202 was established to provide the Marines with a dedicated training squadron. In addition to A-6As and A-6Es, VMAT-202 also flew several TC-4C Academes. In addition, VMAQ-2 flew a few A-6Es along with its EA-6As and EA-6Bs.

In 1990, the Marine Corps embarked on a plan to phase out all of its A-6Es. To trade off the Intruder's long range for the more modern F/A-18D Hornet was a tough decision. The change took place at the rate of one squadron per year between 1990 and 1995. El Toro was the first to relinquish its A-6s, VMA(AW)-121 being followed by VMA(AW)-225 and VMA(AW)-242. The decision to transfer the Marine A-6s to the Navy was intended to alleviate a shortage of A-6s in the fleet caused by wing fatigue and the need to rewing many of the aircraft, as well as to reduce the number of aircraft types in the Corps, thereby reducing the associated operating and training courses.

The first A-6 composite wing aircraft, rebuilt by Naval Aviation Depot (NADEP) Norfolk, was delivered to VA-176 on 4 October 1990. The plan was for all existing A-6Es to be rewinged and given the SWIP improvements simultaneously at the Boeing Wichita facility and at all five NADEPs (formerly Naval Air Rework Facilities). In reality, Boeing only rewinged 11 Intruders, all of which had already received the SWIP improvements at Grumman. As of September 1992, 178 Boeing composite wing kits had been delivered and 136 A-6Es had been modified with both the new wing and the SWIP upgrade at the Norfolk and Alameda NADEPs, as well as the Grumman Calverton and St. Augustine facilities.

The original intent was that all A-6E SWIP aircraft would incorporate the new composite-structure wings, but some of the initial A-6E SWIP Intruders lacked the wing because of the delays in the rewinging program. Therefore, three distinct subvariants existed — A-6E SWIP aircraft with the original metal wing, A-6E SWIP Block I aircraft with the composite wing, and A-6E SWIP Block IA aircraft, also with the composite wing and some improved avionics. The A-6E SWIP aircraft with metal wings were in all other respects identical to A-6E SWIP Block I aircraft with composite wings. The A-6E SWIP Block IA variant, first flown in 1994, incorporated an improved ASN-139 inertial navigation system (INS), ARN-118 TACAN, global positioning system (GPS), and a new heads-up display.

THE END OF A LONG ROAD

The end of the Intruder era came on Thursday, 19 December 1996, when the last operational A-6E was launched from the USS *Enterprise* off the coast of South Carolina. The day was dark and gray, matching the emotions many felt watching the A-6 fly into history. VA-75 had the dubious honor, and the A-6E (BuNo 162179, modex 501) sported nose art of a cartoon boxer on the port side of the radome and the insignia of all Navy Intruder squadrons on its tail. The aircraft was flown by CAPT Bud Jewett and B/N CDR Jim Gagliotti. Retired VADM Richard Allen, who had flown A-6As over Vietnam, gave the wind-up and launch signal as the honorary launch officer. The aircraft recovered at NAS Oceana.

The A-6 had seemed on the verge of retirement before, mainly in the late 1970s and early 1980s when the wing problem became severe and Congress began questioning the need for the aircraft. The Intruders seemed to have been saved when the Navy decided to refit newer models with Boeing composite wings. The original plan indicated that the rewinged aircraft would serve until the year 2000 or slightly later. However, the cancellation of the A-6F and the A-12 left the Navy with some difficult decisions. Finally, in 1993, the Navy decided to retire the A-6 to free up funds for the development and procurement of the F/A-18E/F Super Hornet.

Supporters of the A-6 argued that the Navy could have maintained at least the 174 A-6s that received the new wings, a modification that gained them another 15 or so years of service. The Navy, however, argued that the aging A-6s were too expensive to maintain and were no longer able to penetrate defenses. The premature retirement of the A-6 force effectively left the carrier strike group without an all-weather attack aircraft. In theory the F/A-18D and modified F-14 "Bombcats" picked up the slack, but neither was a truly viable replacement for the A-6E. The Navy would have to wait for the arrival of the F/A-18E/F to have an aircraft that could carry as much ordnance over the same range as the A-6. Eventually, the Joint Strike Fighter will offer a more direct replacement for the A-6E, as well as the Air Forcer A-10 and Marine AV-8 Harrier.

An A-6E being worked on in the hangar bay of the USS John F. Kennedy *during FLEET EX 1-90. Note how the radome opens to allow access to the TRAM and radar equipment. An empty MER is on the inboard pylon.* (U.S. Navy via DVIC)

A CHAF SAFE PIN AND FLAG SWITCH (S6016)

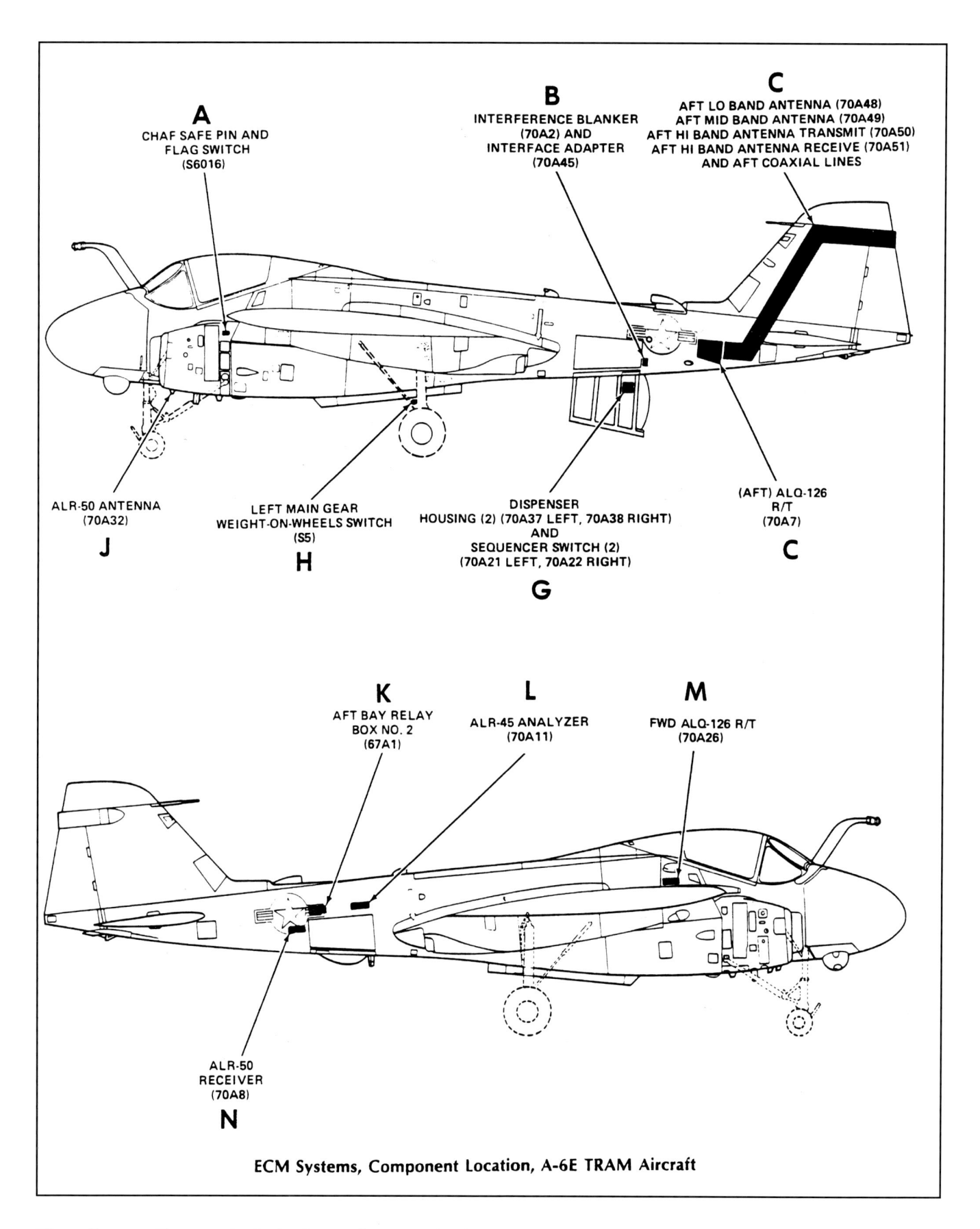

B INTERFERENCE BLANKER (70A2) AND INTERFACE ADAPTER (70A45)

C AFT LO BAND ANTENNA (70A48)
AFT MID BAND ANTENNA (70A49)
AFT HI BAND ANTENNA TRANSMIT (70A50)
AFT HI BAND ANTENNA RECEIVE (70A51)
AND AFT COAXIAL LINES

J ALR-50 ANTENNA (70A32)

H LEFT MAIN GEAR WEIGHT-ON-WHEELS SWITCH (S5)

G DISPENSER HOUSING (2) (70A37 LEFT, 70A38 RIGHT) AND SEQUENCER SWITCH (2) (70A21 LEFT, 70A22 RIGHT)

C (AFT) ALQ-126 R/T (70A7)

K AFT BAY RELAY BOX NO. 2 (67A1)

L ALR-45 ANALYZER (70A11)

M FWD ALQ-126 R/T (70A26)

N ALR-50 RECEIVER (70A8)

ECM Systems, Component Location, A-6E TRAM Aircraft

These diagrams illustrate the final ECM configuration for the A-6E TRAM aircraft — ALQ-126, ALR-45, and ALR-50. The long spoon antennas for the earlier ALQ-100 were deleted from the inboard pylons when the ALQ-126 was fitted. (U.S. Navy)

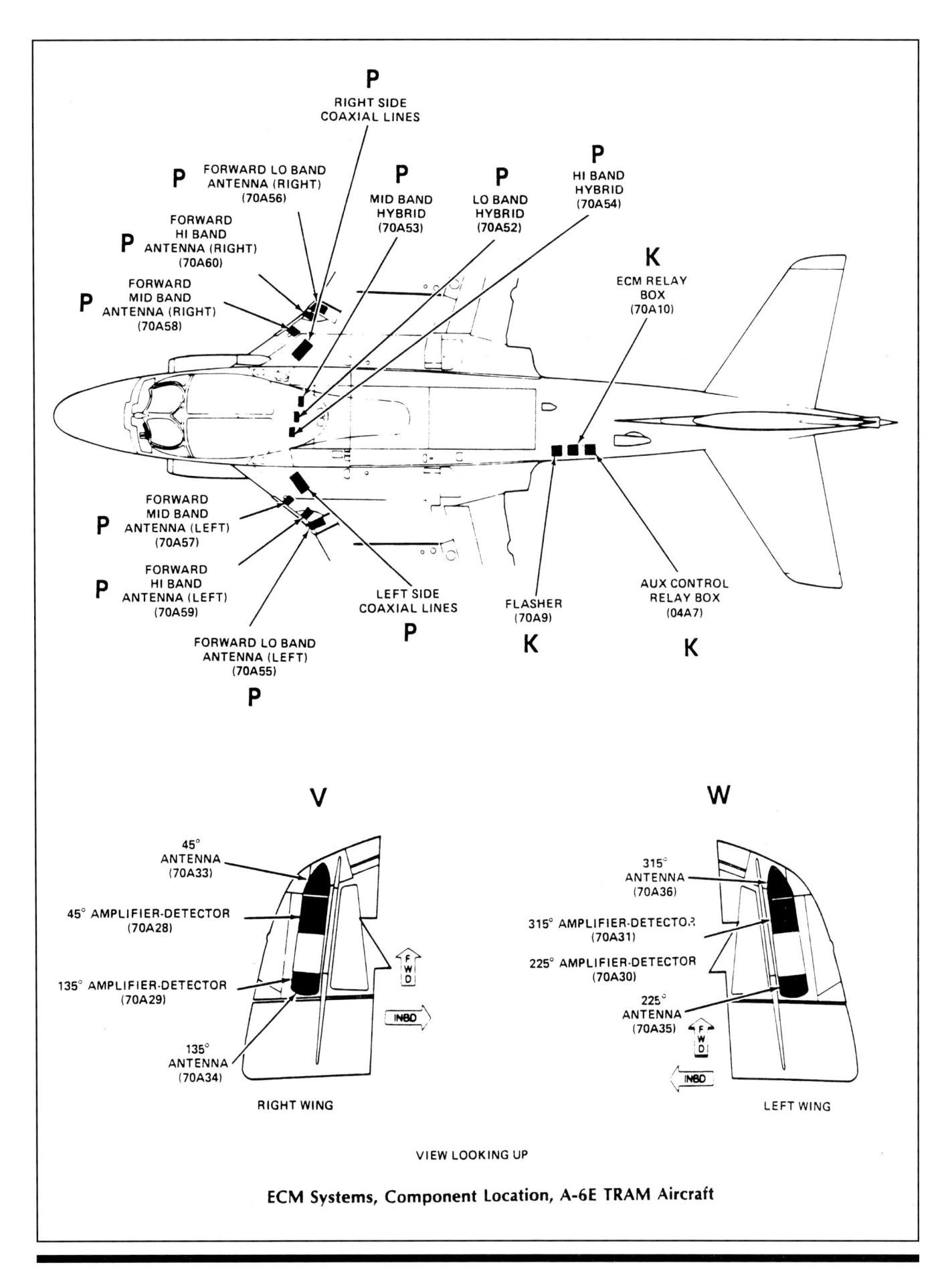

ECM Systems, Component Location, A-6E TRAM Aircraft

GRUMMAN A-6 INTRUDER

The A-6 retirement ceremony was held at NAS Whidbey Island on 27–28 February 1997, and was simulcast via satellite to NAS Oceana. Over 1,000 people attended at Whidbey Island, with an additional 1,800 at Oceana. Three A-6 Intruders flew one last mission over Whidbey Island on 27 February as part of a dedication ceremony honoring the 86 Whidbey crewmen who were killed while flying the A-6, including 11 killed in combat. A ceremony at 1400 hours on the 28th officially retired the Intruders and disestablished VA-196, which had flown more sorties and suffered greater losses than any other carrier-based squadron during the Vietnam War. The last East Coast Intruder squadron, VA-75, was simultaneously disestablished. At Oceana, Secretary of the Navy John Dalton was flanked by two A-6Es — one painted in the 1963 markings used by VA-75 when the A-6A first entered fleet service. Dalton noted that the A-6 was "distinctive looking, some would say 'optically challenged.'" After the ceremony, the remaining Intruders were flown to Davis-Monthan Air Force Base in Tucson, Arizona, for storage and eventual disposition.

During the 34 years that the A-6 was operational, over 2.8 million flight hours had been accumulated. Although possessing a better-than-average accident record for the era, nevertheless 173 pilots and B/Ns lost their lives flying Intruders in combat and accidents.

Interestingly, Intruders would participate in one more mission. In early March 1997, the USS *Dwight D. Eisenhower* (CVN-69) emerged from an 18-month overhaul and needed to recertify its flight deck. On 12 March, the last three remaining A-6Es (BuNos 161662/AA502, 162179/AA501, and 164382/AA500) sortied from NAS Oceana and made a total of 16 traps and 16 cats from the *Eisenhower*.

One hundred low-time rewinged A-6E SWIPs were placed in "war reserve" storage. The Navy also established a program that would allow some of the other rewinged A-6E aircraft to be purchased by friendly nations under the Foreign Military Sales program. Several options existed for these sales — taking the aircraft as-is, having them modified to essentially the A-6G configuration, or other unspecified upgrades. Unfortunately, nobody seemed interested in purchasing an aircraft that had been retired by its only operator, and the A-6s continue to languish at Davis-Monthan. As of the end of 2000 there are still 180 A-6Es at Davis-Monthan, with the oldest arriving on 28 May 1993, and the newest on 26 March 1997. (The last two East Coast Intruders were BuNos 162179 and 164382, arriving on 21 March; the last West Coast aircraft was BuNo 164377, arriving on 26 March.)

REEFS — A-6S UNDERWATER

During 1995 the U.S. Navy joined the fight to help save the wildlife that resides off the coast of Florida. In an attempt to create a new artificial reef, stripped-out A-6 Intruders were sunk about 25 miles off the coast of St. Augustine in about 100 feet of water. The site is called Port Authority Reef Site #9 and includes an old tugboat in addition to the A-6s. On 16 June 1995 the first 26 Intruders were unceremoniously dumped off a barge into the Atlantic; five days later 18 more would follow. A year later a further 26 aircraft were dumped in the same location.

This is not the first time that the state of Florida has attempted to create artificial reefs — in addition to providing a necessary resource for fish, they are a convenient way for scientists to study fish and other sea life up close in semi-controlled environments. Earlier underwater creations utilized such materials as precast concrete, naval vessels, and even old dumpsters.

These A-6Es had been at the Grumman facility in St. Augustine for various conversions (primarily rewinging) when all of the contracts were canceled pending the A-6's removal from service. Instead of allowing the aircraft to rust away without purpose, the state of Florida came through with a use for them.

After the aircraft were dumped into the ocean, divers determined that bait fish arrived within the first few hours, followed by amberjack, king mackerel and barracuda within the first week or so. Within a year, the bottom fish and tiny reef pickers that eat the algae were living there full time. The reef is now an extremely popular location for weekend divers and fishermen.

An A-6E (152941) from VMA(AW)-224 lands at NAF Atsugi, Japan. The aircraft was named "Linda" and carried a small piece of art on the front of the radome — unusual since this location was used to designate EA-6B aircraft to carrier landing signal officers. (Masumi Wada via the Mick Roth Collection)

Intruders from VA-75 on the USS Enterprise *during the A-6's last operational cruise in December 1996. (Robert F. Dorr)*

The cockpit of an A-6E (152630) from VMA(AW)-121 on 1 May 1982. Photographed at MCAS El Toro, California. The pilots' station (above) looks archaic by "glass cockpit" standards, but was in fact very advanced for its time and paved the way for the modern digital displays used in most current aircraft. The small circular scope towards the right side is the radar warning display. (Craig Kaston via the Mick Roth Collection)

Barely discernable in these photos is the fact that the B/N's seat was positioned slightly aft of the pilot's seat in order to provide better visibility for the pilot. The B/N controlled the radar (and later TRIM/TRAM sensors) and armed and dropped the weapons — he had no flight controls and no flight instruments. Although a relatively large aircraft, the A-6 was somewhat cramped in the cockpit, especially for the B/N who had electronic equipment in a wide pedestal between his legs. (Craig Kaston via the Mick Roth Collection)

An A-6E TRAM (162209) from VA-128 photographed at NAS Whidbey Island, on 17 July 1993 . Note the AGM-84 Harpoon missile on the outer wing pylon and the trio of 500-pound bombs on the inboard wing pylon. (Darryl Shaw)

A Northrop BQM-74 target drone is loaded onto an A-6E (159317) at Pt. Mugu. The drone was about as large a store as the A-6 could comfortably carry, and could only be carried on the outer wing pylons. (Northrop via the Tony Thornborough Collection)

Snow! Something not normally associated with Navy aircraft, but not terribly unusual. This A-6E TRAM (160998) from VA-65 was photographed on 11 February 1980. (Katsuhiko Tokunaga via the Mick Roth Collection)

GRUMMAN A-6 INTRUDER

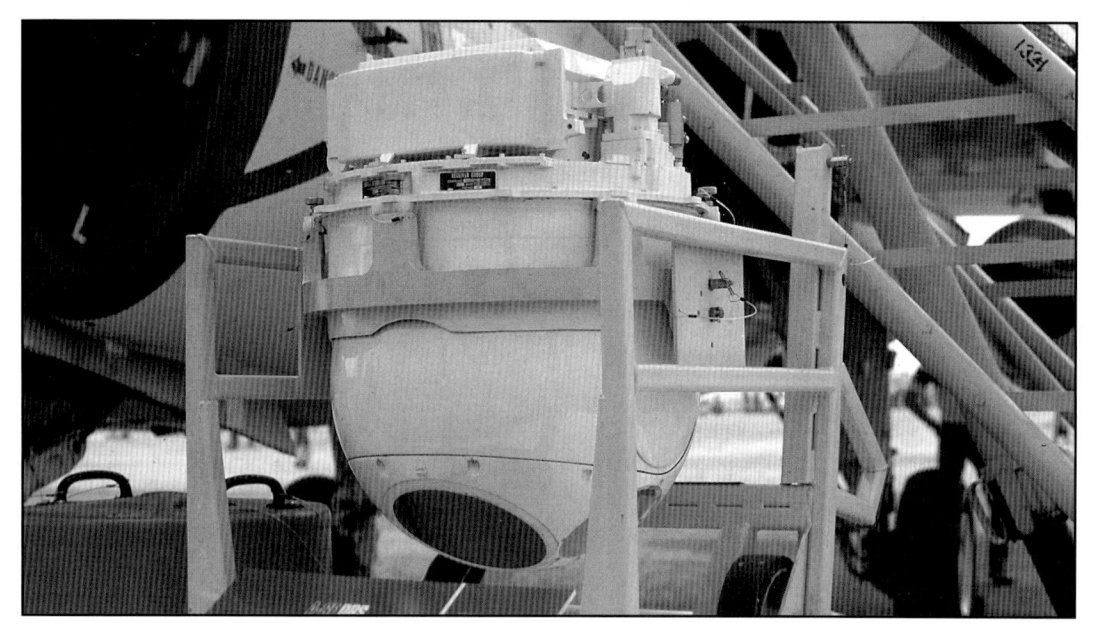

A TRAM turret is displayed outside the aircraft in May 1982. The turret was remarkably compact and fit into the same space as the original tracking radar used on the A-6A (by this time the search and track radars had been combined into a single unit). (Craig Kaston via the Mick Roth Collection)

This A-6E (158795) from VA-75 shows the small AWG-21 antennas under the air intake. A dummy Standard ARM may be seen on the inboard wing pylon. The aircraft was photographed on the USS Saratoga on 8 January 1980. (Robert L. Lawson via the Mick Roth Collection)

This A-6E (158043) from VA-75 carries a load of Mk 82 bombs under the wing, along with a 300-gallon fuel tank on the centerline. Photographed in November 1979. (Michael Grove via the Mick Roth Collection)

THE REPLACEMENT 6

THE STILLBORN A-12 AND A-6F

The Advanced Tactical Aircraft (ATA) program began in 1983 when the Deputy Secretary of Defense directed the Navy to develop a replacement for the A-6 with an initial operational capability of not later than 1994. The program would rely heavily on stealth technology developed by the Air Force, and as such, would become highly-classified and well hidden. In November 1984 teams of McDonnell Douglas/General Dynamics and Northrop/Grumman/Vought were awarded contracts for the concept formulation phase of the ATA development. A little over 18 months later, both teams received contract extensions for the demonstration/validation phase. On 13 January 1988, the General Dynamics/McDonnell Douglas team was announced as the winner and was awarded the full-scale development contract for the newly-designated A-12. The contract was ceiling-priced at $4,800 million and the maiden flight of the first development aircraft was scheduled for December 1990.

The Navy originally planned to buy 620 A-12s, with the Marine Corps purchasing an additional 238 aircraft at an average cost that was estimated at $96.2 million each. At one point the Air Force considered buying an additional 400 derivatives. The A-12 was designed to fly faster and farther than the A-6E, carrying precision-guided weapons internally to reduce drag and maintain a low radar cross-section.

By the beginning of 1990 is was becoming evident to those that were briefed on such things that the A-12 was in serious trouble. Both contractors began reporting new delays, probable cost increases, and business problems to the Navy. The Secretary of Defense, Richard B. Cheney, eliminated the purchase of any Marine Corps aircraft in favor of additional F/A-18D Night Attack Hornets, but emphasized to the contractors that the schedule be maintained. To provide concrete evidence of the Navy's commitment to the program, on 31 May 1990 the Navy exercised a contract option for first production lot of six aircraft at a ceiling price of $1,200 million. However, the next day the Navy leadership was informed of serious development problems by the contractors. As a result, the Department of Defense and Department of Navy ordered investigations into possible fraud and abuse by the contractors.

A report issued on 29 November 1990 detailed wide-ranging A-12 problems that had not been reported to Navy and Pentagon officials. Two weeks later Secretary Cheney told the Navy to "show cause" why the A-12 program should not be canceled — despite a great deal of work on the part of the Navy and the contractors, nobody was convinced. On 7 January 1991, Cheney canceled the program "for default." This was the largest defense program to ever be terminated because the government believed the contractors were either unwilling or incapable of completing the development program. The government ordered the contractors to repay most of the $2,000 million dollars already spent on the program.

In response, McDonnell Douglas and General Dynamics challenged the termination of the contract in the

Everybody is a comedian. The Whidbey Island airshow was the first to display the A-12 — sort of. (Darryl Shaw)

After the A-12 program was cancelled, the full-scale mockup was made public, and was first displayed at the Carswell JRB open house on 29 June 1996. The "flying Dorito," as the A-12 was nicknamed, would have been an interesting sight operating from aircraft carriers. (Greg Fieser)

U.S. Court of Federal Claims. The complaint sought an equitable adjustment of $1,300 million (the so-called "termination penalties") and reimbursement of all costs incurred by the contractors (approximately $2,000 million).

On 19 December 1995, the Court ordered that the government's termination of the A-12 contract "for default" be converted to a termination "for the convenience of the government." On 13 December 1996, the Court issued an opinion confirming its prior no-loss adjustment and no-profit recovery order. This essentially meant that the government could not reclaim the $2,000 million already spent, and would likely have to pay penalties, interest, and court costs. In an early 1997 stipulation, the parties agreed that, based on the prior orders and findings of the court, the companies were entitled to recover $1,071 million. Furthermore, on 22 January 1997, the court issued an opinion in which it ruled that plaintiffs were entitled to recover interest on that amount. The government initially indicated it would appeal the verdict, but the case rapidly faded from sight.

A-6F INTRUDER II

During 1983, Grumman proposed an A-6E Update program that would significantly improve the effectiveness of the Intruder. Despite the fact that the A-12 program was already under way, in June 1984 the Navy awarded a $276 million fixed price development contract for the new A-6F Intruder II. Program managers at Grumman foresaw a threefold increase in survivability with the A-6F, a 20 to 30 percent reduction in maintenance requirements, and fully mission-capable rates of around 70 percent. These improvements would

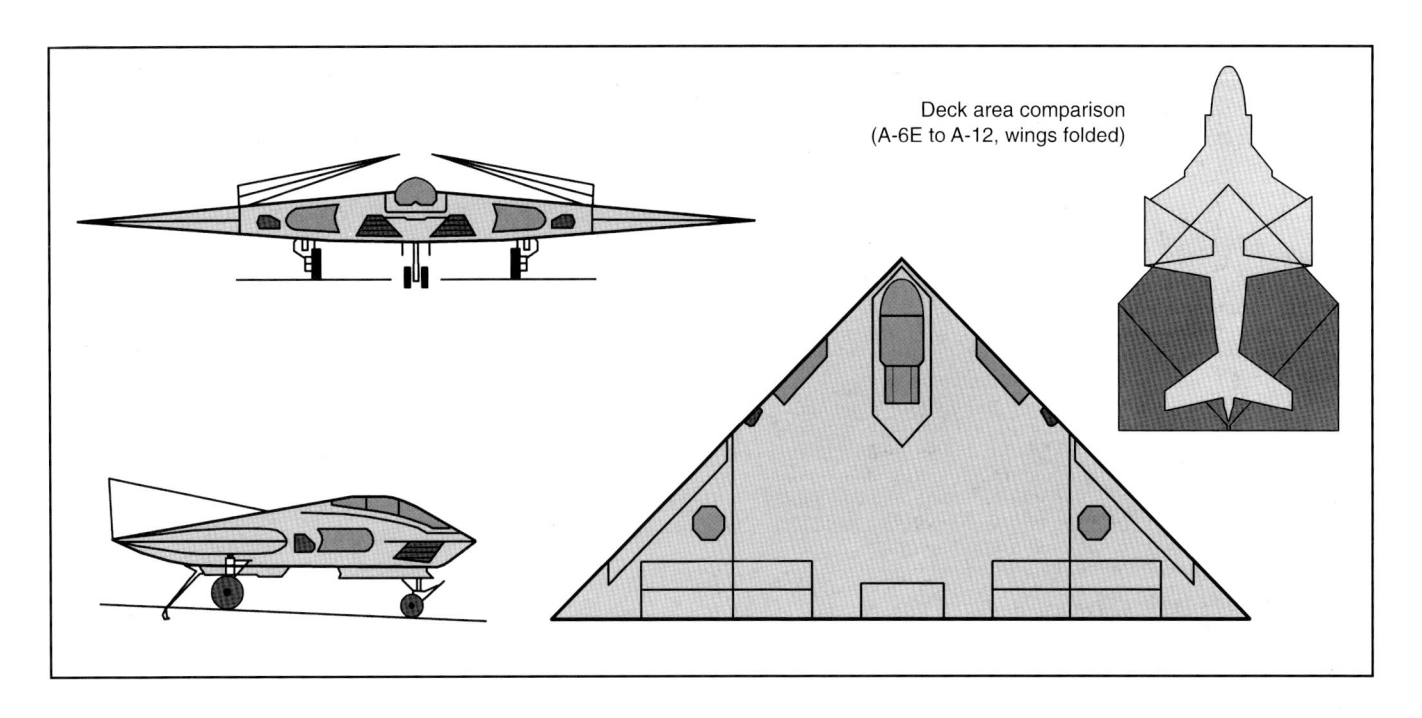

Typical of most early stealth designs, the A-12 was an unconventional shape — in this case a flying triangle. With its wings spread, the Avenger II took considerably more deck space than the A-6 (roughly equivalent to an F-14), but with wings folded it was roughly equivalent to the Intruder. (U.S. Navy)

be coupled with a higher thrust-to-weight ratio from a pair of new engines, along with modern avionics and sensors. The A-6F also included the composite wing developed by Boeing, although an additional stores station was included on each outer wing panel to carry air-to-air missiles

One of the selling points of the program was that the basic airframe remained essentially unchanged, allowing the Navy to modify selected A-6Es to the new configuration in lieu of new procurement. This strategy had worked very successfully with the original A-6E program, the TRAM upgrade, and also on the F-14 program. Initial plans called for a switch to A-6F production in FY88, with the first of 150 new A-6Fs due for delivery in 1989.

Norden Systems was selected to develop the new APQ-173 multimode radar to replace the APQ-148. The new radar featured significantly increased range, standoff weapon integration, inverse synthetic aperture radar capabilities for long-range ship classification, and an air-to-air mode for use with AIM-9L/M Sidewinders or AIM-120 AMRAAM missiles. A decade's worth of state-of-the-art improvements promised significantly improved reliability and lower maintenance. The A-6F would retain the TRAM system without change.

To accommodate the increased information available there would be five "glass" multifunction displays (MFDs) in a totally redesigned cockpit. The pilot would have vertical and horizontal situation displays, while the B/N would have FLIR, radar, and weapons management displays. The MFDs, two AYK-14 tactical computers, ASW-27 two-way data link, and Kaiser Electronics HUDs were common with units installed in the F-14D Tomcat.

Other improvements included an Applied Technology ALR-67 radar warning system, ARC-182 VHF and UHF airborne radios, ARN-118 TACAN, Litton ASN-130 inertial navigation system, ALQ-165 airborne self-protection jammer (ASPJ), replacement of the APN-153 radar altimeter with a Rockwell Collins GPS, improved tactical software, FLIR autotracker for automatic target lock-on and tracking, improved bomb racks, two 40KVA generators, and a windscreen rain removal system. The ALR-67 and ASPJ had already been tested on an A-6E (BuNo 159568) as a possible upgrade to the fleet. The new GPS installation had also already been tested on an A-6E (BuNo 155596) flying back and forth between the USS *America* in the Gulf of Mexico and Patuxent River, Key West, and the Grumman plant in Long Island.

General Electric was selected to provide the 10,800-lbf nonafterburning F404-GE-400D turbofan. The engine was 99 percent common with the afterburning model that powered the

The first two A-6F prototypes (162183 and 162184) fly in formation. The first aircraft did not include the advanced avionics, but the second did. (Grumman via the Robert F. Dorr Collection)

F/A-18A Hornet, and the engine cores were interchangeable with a few hours of work to remove (or install) the afterburner. No modifications were required to the existing A-6 inlets, which provided more airflow than the older J52s ever needed.

As a follow-on, General Electric proposed an augmenter deflector exhaust nozzle (ADEN) version, which could vector the thrust at the exhaust outlet to provide STOL characteristics. These were remarkably similar in concept to the original tilting tailpipes installed on the A2F-1 prototype. The nozzles would allow a 100-knot deck landing speed at an extra 10,000 pounds gross trap or a takeoff run of less than 400 feet at 45,000 pounds gross trap. Unlike the original A2F-1 nozzles, which were hard to distinguish from their fixed replacements, the ADEN nozzles were large rectangular exhausts that extended out from the fuselage approximately two feet. The thrust vector of the system was very close to the A-6 center of gravity. The modification was deemed very low risk and could have begun flight testing within three years of the A-6F service date. The system used a two-dimensional non-axisymmetrical nozzle that had already been tested in engine and altitude test cells. The A-6F was also to carry a Garrett AiResearch auxiliary power unit and an aircraft-mounted accessory drive on each engine.

A revised fuel system with self-sealing armored fuel tanks and void-filling foam between the fuel tanks and airframe, along with a sophisticated fire detection system, contributed to increased battle damage resistance. A total of 15,936 pounds of fuel could be carried in three fuselage and four wing tanks.

The first A-6F (BuNo 162183) made its maiden flight on 26 August 1987 piloted by Gary Hentz and with Dave Goulette in the B/N seat. Developmental work proceeded quickly and the Navy established an F-14D/A-6F joint development office at Patuxent River working toward the goal of having new A-6Fs in the fleet by the early 1990s. By the time the third A-6F (BuNo 162185) flew on 22 August 1988, however, the Navy had already committed to the A-12 program.

Unfortunately, the free-spending days of the Reagan Administration ended as the U.S. economy began to slow down. The Department of Defense decided that the Navy could not sustain two attack aircraft development programs, and against the best advice of several Navy officials, the A-6F program was canceled in favor of continued development of the A-12. The first 30 production A-6Fs (BuNos 163955–163984) had never been started.

A-6G

Following cancellation of the A-6F, plans were made to proceed with the A-6G as a lower-cost alternative; there would be no new-build A-6Gs, only conversions of already rewinged A-6Es. The more modest A-6G program included most of the improvements developed for the A-6F but without the much-needed new engines. The third A-6F prototype had been the first that included the avionics upgrades. This aircraft became the digital systems development (DSD) aircraft for the A-6G.

The first A-6F (162183) shows the extra pylon that was available on the Boeing composite wing — for a total of three per side. The pylon would have been used primarily for light-weight missiles. (Grumman via the Robert F. Dorr Collection)

Several months were spent testing the new radar, avionics, and glass cockpit that were being planned for the A-6G upgrade. However, the Navy could never find the money to properly fund the upgrade and a true A-6G prototype never flew, although the rewinging effort for the existing fleet of A-6Es continued for a while. The rather abrupt decision to retire the A-6Es in the mid-1990s meant that only 174 aircraft received

The Boeing-developed composite wing differed slightly in surface detail. For instance, the wing fold hinge was more flush than on the normal A-6 wing, and a stores pylon was added under the outer panel. (Grumman via the Robert F. Dorr Collection)

the new wing, substantially fewer than the 336 originally anticipated. The fourth and fifth A-6Fs (BuNos 162186 and 162187) were completed, but they were quickly mothballed and never flown.

Final production of the A-6 amounted to 701 aircraft, not including the EA-6As and EA-6Bs. This consisted of 8 prototype A-6As (sometimes called YA-6As), 480 A-6As, 97 new-build A-6Es, 69 new-build A-6E TRAMs, 34 new-build A-6E SWIPs, and 5 prototype A-6Fs. The last 19 A-6E SWIPs and all 5 A-6Fs were equipped with the Boeing composite wing on the production line. The A-6A series contained 13 aircraft converted to EA-6As, 19 A-6B conversions, and 12 A-6Cs. One other A-6A had been converted into the lone JA-6A, two others became NA-6A test beds, and several others were used extensively for tests, including as prototypes for the A-6B and A-6C configurations. A total of 78 A-6As and 16 A-6Es were converted to KA-6Ds. The three prototype EA-6Bs started life as A-6As, as did 241 A-6Es that were converted from A-6As.

STILLBORN VARIANTS

As with any aircraft that enjoyed a long and successful service career, there were various proposals generated for other variants of the aircraft that never made production. A few of the Intruder's lesser-known concepts follow.

Single-Seater. This aircraft would have been optimized for daylight visual attack, generally along the lines of the A-7 Corsair II. Almost all of the advanced avionics were removed, the forward fuselage was reshaped to provide a single-seat cockpit and no radome, and the wings and horizontal stabilizer were designed to fold near the fuselage to allow for very high-density storage aboard a carrier. With the A-7 already in production — and little commonality with the existing A-6A — there was really no reason for the Navy to pursue this design, and it did not.

Air Force. Intruders configured for Air Force service were proposed at least twice — once in 1958 and again around 1963. The second time the concept advanced far enough that the aircraft apparently received the A-6B designation, although it could not be ascertained if this was ever officially granted or simply speculation on the part of Grumman. The designation was subsequently reused for a modified A-6A variant. Typical of Navy aircraft converted for Air Force service, this version replaced most of the Navy-specific

The first A-6F (162183) on its maiden flight on 26 August 1987 piloted by Gary Hentz and with Dave Goulette in the B/N seat. Note the long flight test instrumentation boom on the nose. (Grumman via the Robert F. Dorr Collection)

The third A-6F had a complete set of avionics and the new composite wing. After the A-6F program was cancelled in favor of the A-12, Grumman pitched the A-6G — essentially an A-6F without the new turbofan engines. The third A-6F (162185) was used as a digital systems development (DSD) aircraft for the A-6G before that program was also cancelled due to fiscal constraints. (Grumman via the Robert F. Dorr Collection)

avionics (radios, etc.) with Air Force units, added an Air Force-style refueling system, and deleted the folding wing provisions. No other information seems to have been made public about the aircraft.

Air Force Tanker. This was an even more bizarre concept. Given the relative success of the KA-6D, Grumman investigated adding an Air Force-style refueling boom under the nose of an A-6 to provide a small-size tanker for the Air Force. A long boom also extended from the nose that was equipped with refueling position lights to give the approaching aircraft the same reference queues provided by the lights under the KC-135. The aft-facing boom operator sat in the mid-fuselage location usually used by the birdcage. With a large supply of KC-135 tankers at hand, the Air Force expressed little interest in the concept.

Armed Tanker. This was essentially a standard KA-6D equipped with a 20mm cannon in the nose and would have provided a slightly increased attack capability for an aircraft that lacked most of the ability of its combat cousins. The Navy looked at various implementations of this idea for a few years before finally deciding to delete all of the attack capabilities from later KA-6Ds.

Intruders with Guns. A total of 18 different designs were evaluated by Grumman that added a cannon to the basic A-6 design. Mounting locations included the wing roots, under the fuselage, in the forward fuselage, and under the wings. One design even included a centerline-mounted rotating turret. Various 20mm and 30mm cannon were considered, with the favorite being the British-designed ADEN 30mm unit. The designs featured between 100 and 1,500 rounds of ammunition per gun. A truly workable design was never found, and the Navy expressed little interest in the concept anyway, so the idea was finally dropped from consideration.

Missileer Intruder. The Navy had always wanted a fleet defense aircraft and had almost managed to get one with the F6D Missileer and the XAAM-10 Eagle missile. When this aircraft was canceled, the Navy briefly looked at equipping an A-6 variant with the large radar and missile package since it would have fit fairly easily into the airframe. The basic setup for the Intruder was similar to that planned for the F6D — three missiles under each wing, with the possibility of a seventh carried on the centerline. The weight of this load severely hampered the performance of the Intruder, and some consideration was given to fitting a suitable turbofan powerplant (probably a variant of the TF30) and larger wings. The concept was quietly dropped shortly thereafter. Eventually, the radar and missile were morphed into the AWG-9 and AIM-54 Phoenix used on the Navy/Grumman F-14 Tomcat.

Phoenix Intruder. Well, maybe the concept was not completely dropped. As the price of the new F-14 continued to climb, Grumman briefly investigated arming a modified A-6 with the AWG-9 and Phoenix in a concept that looked remarkably like the Missileer proposal. The wings would have been extended four feet, while the fuselage grew five feet in length mainly to compensate for center of gravity changes. The Navy really wanted F-14s instead, and eventually found a way to afford them.

Recce Intruder. Almost every decent tactical fighter/bomber/attack aircraft gets considered for a reconnaissance role, and the A-6 was no exception. Most early ideas involved fitting a camera package into the mid-fuselage birdcage and tuning the radars for better resolution for ground mapping. One later proposal used a four-seat aircraft that looked remarkably like the eventual EA-6B and included an advanced side-looking radar. Reportedly this concept received the RA-6A designation, but no official confirmation could be found.

Three-Seat A-6. Although a two-seat aircraft, the A-6 cockpit arrangement did not lend itself well as a trainer. This version would have added a third seat above and between the two existing seats to accommodate a safety pilot. This would have allowed the two regular crewmen to concentrate on training each other (the normal pilot could act as an instructor for the B/N, or vice versa). The TC-4C Academe was purchased instead.

Heavy-Weight Intruder. Grumman flirted with an idea that would have allowed the A-6 to carry two 10,000-pound Mk 121 demolition bombs. These weapons were over four feet in diameter and nearly 19 feet long. Although ways were found to physically fit the bombs to the airframe, the available power prohibited operations from carriers, largely negating any benefit to the idea. In fact, the only aircraft that ever successfully deployed the weapons were modified C-130s that rolled them out of the rear cargo doors.

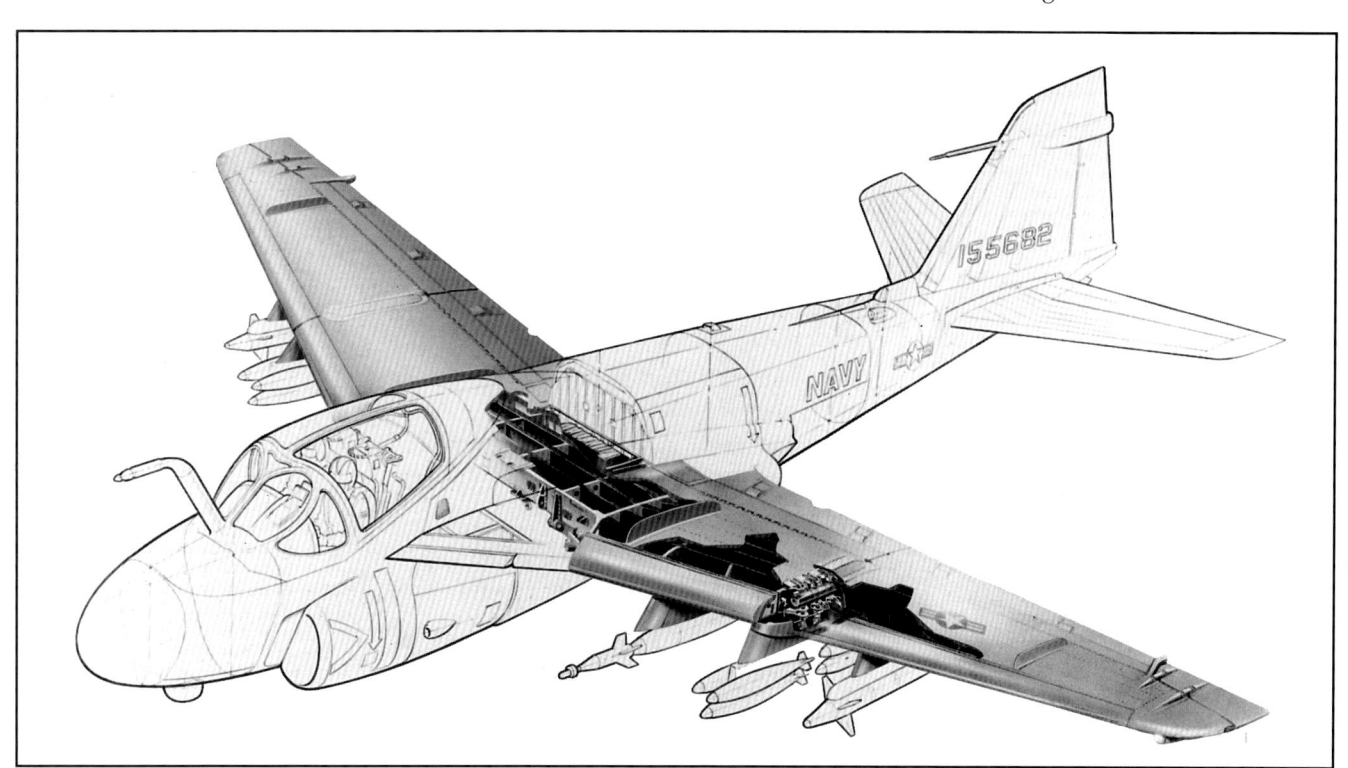

The Boeing-developed composite wing promised to significantly extend the service life of the A-6E/F/G models, but was actually installed on very few aircraft before the Intruder was retired. (Grumman via the Robert F. Dorr Collection)

BUREAU NUMBERS

RETS, BACS, MODS, AND OTHERS

BuNos	Qty	Designation/Notes
147864 – 147867	4	A2F-1
148615 – 148618	4	A2F-1
149475 – 149486	12	A-6A
149935 – 149958	24	A-6A
151558 – 151600	43	A-6A
151601 – 151612		A-6A Cancelled
151780 – 151827	48	A-6A
152583 – 152646	64	A-6A
152891 – 152954	64	A-6A
152955 – 152964		A-6A Cancelled
154046 – 154099		A-6A Cancelled
154124 – 154171	48	A6A
155137 – 155190		A-6A Cancelled
155581 – 155721	141	A-6A
156994 – 157029	36	A-6A
158041 – 158052	12	A-6E
158053 – 158072		KA-6D Cancelled
158528 – 158539	12	A-6E
158787 – 158798	12	A-6E
159174 – 159185	12	A-6E
159309 – 159317	9	A-6E

BuNos	Qty	Designation/Notes
159567 – 159581	15	A-6E
159895 – 159906	12	A-6E
160421 – 160431	11	A-6E
160993 – 160994	2	A-6E
160995 – 160998	4	A-6E TRAM
161082 – 161093	12	A-6E TRAM
161100 – 161111	12	A-6E TRAM
161112 – 161114		A-6E Cancelled
161230 – 161235	6	A-6E TRAM
161236 – 161241		A-6E Cancelled
161659 – 161690	32	A-6E TRAM
161691 – 161694		A-6E Cancelled
161886 – 161897		A-6E Cancelled
162179 – 162181	3	A-6E TRAM
162182	1	A-6E SWIP
162183 – 162187	5	A-6F (composite wing)
162188 – 162201	14	A-6E SWIP
162202 – 162210	9	A-6E SWIP (composite)
162211 – 162222		A-6E Cancelled
163955 – 163984		A-6F Cancelled
164376 – 164385	10	A-6E SWIP (composite)

A-6As converted to A-6Es

BuNos	Qty
149948 – 149950	3
149953	1
149955 – 149957	3
151558	1
151562	1
151564 – 151565	2
151573	1
151591 – 151593	3
151782	1
151784	1
161790	1
151802	1
151804	1
151807	1
151811 – 151812	2
151814	1
151820	1
152583 – 152585	3
152587	1
152591	1
152593	1
152596	1
152599 – 152600	2
152603	1
152607	1

BuNos	Qty
152610	1
152614	1
152617	1
152620 – 152621	2
152623	1
152630	1
152634 – 152635	2
152640 – 152642	3
152645	1
152895	1
152902	1
152904 – 152905	2
152907 – 152908	2
152912	1
152915 – 152916	2
152918	1
152923 – 152925	3
152928 – 152931	4
142933	1
152935 – 152936	2
152941	1
152945	1
152947 – 152948	2
152950	1
152953 – 152954	2
154124	1
154126	1

BuNos	Qty
154128 – 154129	2
154131 – 154132	2
154134 – 154137	4
154140	1
154142	1
154144	1
154146	1
154148	1
154151	1
154154	1
154156	1
154158 – 154159	2
154161 – 154163	3
154167 – 154171	5
155581	1
155585 – 155586	2
155588 – 155592	5
155595 – 155600	6
155602	1
155604	1
155606	1
155608	1
155610	1
155612	1
155615 – 155617	3
155619 – 155621	3
155623 – 155625	3

BuNos	Qty
155627 – 155633	7
155625 – 155638	14
155642 – 155646	5
155648 – 155649	2
155651	1
155653 – 155662	10
155664 – 155665	2
155667 – 155670	4
155672 – 155676	5
155678 – 155685	8
155687 – 155689	3
155692	1
155694 – 155695	2
155697 – 155699	3
155702 – 155704	3
155706 – 155708	3
155710 – 155719	10
156995 – 156997	3
157000 – 157006	7
157009 – 157014	6
157016 – 157017	2
157019	1
157021	1
157023 – 157027	5
157029	1

GRUMMAN A-6 INTRUDER

SIGNIFICANT DATES

KEY DATES IN THE HISTORY OF THE A-6 INTRUDER

1956
The Navy conducts a long-range objectives (LRO) study for the next-generation attack aircraft.

2 October 1956
The Chief of Naval Operation issues an operational requirement (CA-01504) for the new aircraft.

5 March 1957
The Navy announces a design competition for the a attack aircraft.

16 August 1957
The aerospace industry submits proposals to the Navy for the new attack aircraft.

2 January 1958
Grumman is named as the winner of the competition.

14 February 1958
Grumman receives a $3,410,148 contract for the design of the A2F-1 Intruder and the construction of a full-scale mockup.

26 March 1959
A $101 million development contract is awarded to Grumman for eight YA2F-1 prototypes plus detailed engineering.

19 April 1960
The first YA2F-1 makes its maiden flight from Calverton, NY, with Bob Smyth at the controls.

18 September 1962
The A2F-1 is redesignated A-6A under the new uniform DoD designation scheme.

1 February 1963
Vice Admiral Frank O'Breirne took formal delivery of the first two operational A-6As and issued them to attack squadron VA-42.

1 July 1965
Navy A-6As join in attacks against North Vietnam. It was the beginning of a long involvement in Southeast Asia for the Intruder.

March 1967
The first launch of an AGM-78 Standard ARM from an A-6.

14 June 1967
The first TC-4C Academe made its maiden flight from Calverton.

22 August 1967
The first of ten A-6Bs was redelivered to the Navy.

November 1967
The first PAT/ARM trials are accomplished using an A-6A.

December 1967
Marine Corps A-6As join the fight over Vietnam.

26 August 1968
The first A-6B PAT/ARM makes its initial flight.

25 February 1970
The first fully-equipped A-6C was redelivered after having made its maiden flight on 11 June 1969.

27 February 1970
The prototype A-6E makes its maiden flight at Calverton.

16 April 1970
The first converted KA-6D makes its maiden flight at Calverton.

30 April 1970
The first TIAS A-6B was redelivered to the Navy.

December 1970
The last of 480 A-6As (not counting the eight YA2F-1s) rolls off the production line.

17 September 1971
The first new-production (not converted) A-6E is delivered to the Navy.

18 June 1972
VA-145 begins trials of the Air Force AVQ-10A PAVE KNIFE pod on modified A-6As.

16 April 1973
The first converted (CILOP) A-6E is redelivered to the Navy.

1976
The A-6E TRAM is introduced.

26 August 1987
The first A-6F makes its maiden flight; unfortunately the program is cancelled a year later.

19 December 1996
The last operational A-6E catapult takes place off the USS *Enterprise*.

27-28 February 1997
The A-6 retirement ceremony is held at Whidbey Island and Oceana; the A-6 is withdrawn from the Navy inventory.